Improvise to Success!

16 Simple but Powerful Principles from Improv Comedy that will take you to Personal and Professional Success!

Copyright Info

Other Stuff
By Avish Parashar

DVDs:
Improv for Speakers!
Improv for Consultants!
Improv for Authors!

For more DVDs and info, visit:
www.ImprovForEveryone.com

Books:
Supercharge Your Creativity!
124 Tips to Develop and Apply Your Creativity
(tips booklet)

For More Products, visit:
www.AvishParashar.com

Thanks

Many people have helped me put this book together. Not only in the specific act of the writing, but also in the years preceding when many of the ideas and principles were being (slowly) formulated. I am sure I am leaving some deserving people off, and if so, please accept my deepest apologies.

Kirstin, Steve, Kathy, thanks for making sure I actually wrote this and keeping me going with encouragement of a kick in the butt!

Thanks to Ed and Fred for your help, advice, and for keeping me going in this business.

Thanks to everyone in NSA, Full Circle, Toastmasters, NetIP and Polywumpus for supporting and helping me along the way.

Thanks to Jennifer Phillips for being a great friend and being an amazing graphic designer.

I would like to thank my friends Mike, Kendall, Alex, Craig, Dave, Nye, and Terry for keeping me on course and keeping me a bit crazy.

Dedication

This book is dedicated to my family for believing in and supporting me over all these years.

Table of Contents

Introduction

Improv Comedy???

The first reaction people have to the idea of applying improv comedy to their professional or personal lives is, "Come on now, life is serious. How can improv comedy apply to that?"

This response is more than a little surprising for the simple reason that *we all improvise every second of every day!* Oh, we all love to try to control life and the world around us, but ultimately we are all making it up as we go along. Once in rare while things will go as planned, but more often than not the universe will throw us a curve ball that we have to deal with on the spot.

Therefore, it stands to reason that if we are improvising every second of every day, then by understanding the principles of great improvisation we can understand the principles of a great life.

The keys to successful improv are the willingness to take risks, the understanding of how to tap into your own creative resources, and the ability to listen to and work well with other people. Show me a person in the whole wide world who wouldn't benefit from having a willingness to take risks, the ability to tap into his creativity, and the skill to listen and work with others.

An improviser must constantly take risks. The primary risk is stepping on stage with nothing prepared and trying to create something entertaining. Without embracing this risk, the improviser does nothing. In a similar fashion, anyone who wants to grow and move forward (which really should be everyone) must push forward and try new ideas and methods. Without risk, there is no progress or innovation.

Creativity is often misconstrued as 'artistry.' In improv, it is clear that the performer needs to be creative. An improviser needs to generate interesting ideas immediately, without a moment's hesitation. While most artistic people are creative, creativity is about much more than art. Creativity is simply the ability to create. It is the ability to come up with something from nothing. It is the ability to create new ideas. These new ideas could be solutions to problems, innovative new ideas, or new ways of handling difficult people. Just because artists are creative doesn't mean that non-artists can't benefit from their own creativity.

Unlike stand-up comedy, where the performer is alone, improv requires cooperation between two or more players. When one performer ignores his partners and does not involve them at all, he creates a disharmonious environment that tears at the group. The best improv happens when everyone is involved and there is a free flow of ideas that are supported and built upon by everyone. This attitude is the heart of communication. Whether talking to a co-worker, client, friend, or family member, the ability to openly and honestly listen to other people and incorporate their ideas is the key to building strong relationships.

The keys to effective improvisation are the same as the keys to success in just about any other area of life. It really should not be that surprising though; life, after all, is the ultimate improvisation.

What is Improv?

Improv comedy is a form of theater where the performers take the stage with nothing prepared and make up instant comedy based on the audience's suggestions. Contrary to popular opinion, improv comedy is not standup. Rather than one performer with a microphone telling jokes, improv consists of a group of performers working together to create improvised scenes on the spot. Improv requires teamwork and creativity, and, when done properly, is hilarious, energetic, and fun for performers and audiences alike!

However, there are many variations on this basic scene. Players can be restricted in what they say or how they move. They can be forced to act things out with certain emotions or in specific genres. They may be forced to work together in unusual ways (one player can act as the 'arms' of another, for example).

If you have ever seen the Drew Carey hosted the television show, 'Whose Line Is It Anyway?', then you have seen improv comedy.

In case you have never seen an improv comedy show, here are examples of some games an improv group might play:

Scenes Without the Letter _____ - The players are forced to act out a scene without using a specified letter of the alphabet in any word they say. If they accidentally use a word, they are removed from the scene and replaced with another player.

Yes And - Two participants have a conversation where every sentence must begin with the phrase 'Yes, and....' By starting every sentence this way, the players agree with their partners, and then build off of what they said.

Expert Interview - A player is assigned a topic on which to be an expert. The trick is, the topic will be something on which the player is most assuredly _not_ an expert! The remaining participants then ask the expert questions on the topic, which he must answer without hesitation.

Bonus Improv Exercises On-Line

Each of the principles in this book comes from the world of improv comedy. One of the best ways to learn the principles is to play the improv games. It is one thing to read about something, or even hear or see it, but it is entirely another to experience it. Not only will you be practicing valuable skills, but you will also have a lot of fun.

For a **FREE** downloadable guide to over 25 practice exercises and improv games, complete with the point of the game, explanation of how to play, tips to make it better, and takeaway points, visit:

www.AvishParashar.com/bookbonus

The key with the exercises is to have fun and not get too stressed out over them. You will make mistakes; you will do it wrong; but that's the way you learn and get better.

The exercises are also designed to be silly and weird. Don't let that throw you. By making them silly they become fun. But the silliness will also take some pressure off. If you are playing something crazy, you can't get too upset or stressed if you mess up, right?

Thanks for reading!
Avish

Principle #1:

Have Fun!

Having fun! Sounds great, doesn't it? And yet, having fun is one of the first things most people forget about as they go through life.

When teaching improv comedy, I am constantly reminding people to have fun. Improv, after all, is a silly art form, and when people take it too seriously the performance suffers.

In the struggle to "get it right," most beginning performers forget all about having fun. They obsess over the rules and techniques. I actually find the easiest way to improve a beginner's performance is to call out, "have more fun!" The mentality often is, "when I get it down and do well, then it will be fun." Amazingly, the opposite is true. When you have fun, you will start to get it down and do well.

This paradigm works in life as well. Most people believe that things will be fun once they "make it." This is unfortunate because the way it usually works is that the more fun you have now, the more likely you are to make it. Yes, things get even better later on, but you'll never get there if it's all struggle.

Somewhere along the way, most of us learned to "be serious." Among school, home, and work, we were taught that having fun was not what it was all about. It was far more important to "be responsible." Work and school were the times to be serious, and playtime was the time to have fun.

This is an incredibly unfortunate mentality to have. Think about it. If you work 40 hours a week, then that consists of about 50% of your waking hours. Between commuting and extra work, most people spend more than 40 hours per week. It seems like a crime to let more than half of your waking life be devoid of fun just because you have an idea that work is not a time for fun.

This seems obvious. There are plenty of people out there talking about doing what you love, and finding your passion. But if you look around, people everywhere are not having any fun! What's that all about?!?

What is Fun?

Let me make one thing clear. I hate people who are always "on." You know exactly whom I am talking about: the "comedian" who makes light of everything or the person who goofs off and misses deadlines. While I believe having fun is a number one priority, I do not advocate being irresponsible or insensitive. When I say "have fun," I mean for you to make sure that you enjoy what you do. Approach your life, work, and relationships with a smile. Look for ways to have fun and laugh, but do it within the context of doing what is right and responsible.

The key is to have fun *doing what you are doing.* The person who thinks he is having fun while slacking off is avoiding life. It's not about going to work and taking excessive lunches and breaks, or chatting everyone's ear off. It's really about finding ways of making the work you do fun.

You might be thinking, "Well my job is terrible – there's no way to have fun at what I do." If that's true, you have two choices: 1) find a way, or 2) move on!

Inertia

Newton's 1st Law of Thermodynamics is that a body at rest tends to stay at rest. This principle is the biggest reason why many people don't have fun. It's always easier to stay as you are than to change!

If your life is not fun, you will need to exert a little effort to find ways of making it fun. You can no longer shuffle in to work and do things the exact same way you have been doing them. The changes don't need to be huge, but they do need to happen. For example, can you listen to a radio or iPod while you work? Can you restructure when you work on things to get your high-stress items done first so you can feel good the rest of the day? Can you arrange your desk or schedule to avoid the annoying person at work?

The answers may not come immediately, and you must be willing to overcome inertia if you want to start having more fun.

Of course, if you really think about it and realize that you just can't have fun at work (maybe the person you work with directly everyday is awful; or maybe you just don't like the actual work you have to do), you should consider looking for something new. This requires overcoming a great deal of inertia, which is why so many people stay at unfulfilling jobs for so long. Many employers realize this and keep giving incentives for employees such as stock options, 401K's, retirement funds, and regular promotions. On a positive note, these sorts of things are designed to reward employees for loyalty and service, and to give them a vested interest in the company's success. On a negative note, they are designed to encourage people to remain with the company even if the work is not enjoyable. Consider this though – time is the only irreplaceable commodity! You may love your income, options, and funds, and leaving may set you back. But you can always earn more. What you can never replace is the time you spend not enjoying life.

Inertia may be the single biggest destroyer of hopes and dreams. If you are not having fun and enjoying what you are doing (in or out of work), overcome that inertia and change it!

Why This is Important

Life is too short to not have fun. If you are willing to throw away 50% of your waking hours, then that's really too bad. But having fun isn't just a "quality of life" principle. It's a great performance principle too.

I don't mean "performance" in the sense of theater or improv. I mean it in the sense of how well you perform at the things you do in your life. The more fun you have the better you will do.

Think about something in your life that you do very well. Chances are, you also enjoy doing it (if not, then I am guessing that you used to enjoy doing it, and for whatever reason you are now burned out on it). Also chances are that you enjoyed the process of getting better at it. While I'm sure there was work and effort, overall, I'm confident that you enjoyed the process itself.

The more fun you have and the more enjoyable you find what you do, the better you will be at it and the more success you will find. It's just that simple, but because we have conditioned ourselves to think that work = serious, most of us never embrace this simple, yet powerful, idea.

Stephen King has a great bit of advice on this topic: "Ask yourself frequently, 'am I having fun?' The answer needn't always be yes. But if it's always no, it's time for a new project or a new career."

How to Have Fun

So right now you may be thinking, "Ok, that's all fine and good. But how do you expect me to have fun when bad things happen, or when I have an awful job?" Here's the first answer to that: It is never the things outside of us that dictate how we feel, but rather our responses to them.

You probably know some people who can always keep their chins up and maintain a positive outlook no matter what is happening. You probably also know some people who seem to look at everything in a negative light. If you showed people from both groups the exact same situation, they would probably offer up two completely different interpretations of the situation. All of the difference is in how you perceive things! To get a bit

"The more fun you have and the more enjoyable you find what you do, the better you will be at it and the more success you will find"

philosophical for a second, there is no reality, there is only perception. All of our own realities are in our minds, because we perceive reality through our own filters.

Ok, back to earth here. What this comes down to is that rather than taking a situation and calling it "good" or 'bad" and letting that affect you, you are much better served to "find the good" or "find the fun" in any situation.

We all know people who can always find a reason to complain. If they get new and better jobs, they focus on how hard it is to switch jobs. When they get into a relationship they focus on what's wrong with the other people, or how the relationships will end. Rather than pursuing their dreams they focus on how they will never happen.

If negative people can find the negative in anything, why can't you choose to find the positive in anything? You can, and here are a few ways to make sure you are having fun and staying positive in your life:

What is Your Focus?

The fastest way to bring yourself around to being positive and having fun is to control your focus. Remember, reality is what you perceive. What you perceive is based on what your focus is.

Negative people find themselves (or force themselves) to focus on the negatives; positive people focus on the positives. If you want to have fun, focus on what's fun in a situation. One of the smarmiest clichés out there is, "positive people take the sunshine with them!" Smarmy though it may be, it does offer up a nice way of looking at focus.

If you are going on an outdoor picnic and it starts to rain, how do you react? The negative person focuses on the rain and how the entire day is ruined. The positive person focuses on figuring out ways of having fun despite the weather. Who would you rather be? Who would you rather be around?

Imagine that a loved one is in the hospital. On what do you focus? Many people focus on the worst case scenario and get stressed and depressed. By doing this they feel that they are exerting some form of control of the situation ("If I'm stressed I'm doing something!"). Others react by focusing on the best case scenario, such as a successful procedure, a speedy recovery, etc. They don't diminish the danger, they do take whatever steps and preparations are needed, but they don't obsess over it.

To the negative, stressed person, the positive person appears to be taking the situation lightly. This is not the case at all. The positive person realizes one important point: *whether you focus on the positive or the negative, in that situation whatever will happen will happen*. No one is influencing anything by focusing on the negative or the positive.

A friend went through a situation like this and he said something very profound (he was refusing to get depressed when his wife was diagnosed with a brain tumor and was going in for surgery in a few weeks). He said, "If the absolute worst comes to pass, I don't want to have our last few weeks together to be all depressed and weepy. I want us to spend our time laughing and joking and enjoying each other like we always have."

That's a pretty amazing attitude. If he can take that approach with a wife going in for brain surgery, do you think you could apply the same approach to all those little things that stress you out?

(Note: The procedure was done successfully – see, worrying would have accomplished nothing!)

Questions

The easiest way to direct your focus is to adjust the questions you are asking yourself. Instead of asking, "What's going to go wrong today?" ask, "What can I enjoy about today?"

Instead of focusing on the problem ("This is terrible!"), focus on the solution (ask, "How can we solve this problem?")

Shift your focus from blame to resolution (Instead of, "Who's fault is this?" ask, "What can we do to fix this?")

Change from asking "Why does this always happen?" to "What can I do to make sure this doesn't happen again?"

Ask yourself simple things like, "What's funny about this?" or "How can I make this fun?"

27

Your brain is immensely powerful. By asking these questions you shift your focus and improve your approach. And chances are your brain will start giving you good answers to those questions.

Play More!

Yes, you should play more! You should play at work as well, not just when you leave. As kids, we had it right! A kid basically has one purpose – to play as much as possible. As adults, we lose that attitude and approach, which is really sad. Find ways of "playing" in whatever you do and you will have fun and be more effective.

I am not saying that you should take this to the extreme – don't show up at work with a baseball and bat and turn the office into a ballgame! And don't play in a way that reduces other people's productivity or offends them.

But can you add some humor into the workday? Can you create some friendly competition (keyword: "friendly"!)? Can you turn work activities into "games" that become more fun to do? Can you work in a group with people you enjoy instead of keeping your head buried in your cubicle?

The rule of thumb is to work first, play second. This is a fine rule and a necessary one to make sure that what needs to get done gets done. But I say why not work first and play first?

Be Enthusiastic and Passionate

What's amazing about the world is how annoyed society seems to get at people who are doing it right! Have you been around someone who is incredibly enthusiastic? It's usually a very good and engaging thing. But if you look around at others, they sometimes get annoyed by people who are enthusiastic. It's almost like they are saying, "What's she got going on to be so enthusiastic about?" What happens is on some level they are jealous of people who have some kind of passion in their lives.

My advice is ignore the naysayers! Enthusiasm is a great thing and an absolute must if you want to have fun and succeed! You have two options to create enthusiasm: 1) Do things you are already passionate about, or 2) Find ways to feel passionate about the things you are already doing.

Obviously, the first option is easier. However, it can be hard to find opportunities to do what you love (especially if you are trying to make it your vocation). Don't give up though, and don't assume you can't find ways of doing it. If you are enthusiastic enough and focus, your enthusiasm will give you the energy to find a way.

> *"Enthusiasm is a great thing and an absolute must if you want to have fun and succeed!"*

You can also find ways of weaving your enthusiasm into things. For example, I love speaking in public. It's my career now, but even before that I would volunteer (at first, and then it just became expected of me) to make announcements and short speeches at events. I was often the "spokesperson" when doing group work and presentations. This was a way of taking what I was enthusiastic about and adding it into my day.

The second option is a little more challenging, but, with the right focus, it can be done. Think about your primary work activity – what do you spend most of your time working on each day? Are you enthusiastic about it? If not, then I would highly suggest you find ways of getting enthusiastic about it.

How do you do this? The first way is to control your focus. When you are doing your work, on what are you focusing? Is your mind wrapped around how you wish you were doing something else, or how you can't wait to leave to go home? If so, you will never get a sense of enthusiasm. First, retrain your thinking to focus on what you do like about what you are doing and what benefits you get from this work.

Second, determine if you can modify the activity so that it is more fun. I once needed to do some mindless data entry, working at home, and I was not enthusiastic about it at all! I was into hardcore procrastinating mode at that point. What got me through it was when I realized that the task was mindless enough that it didn't really require that much attention, I moved a TV into my work area and watched movies during the day while entering the data. Now I wasn't doing just a mindless task. I was watching movies for fun while being necessarily productive!

You may not be able to roll a TV into your office, but you may be able to modify what you do. As I mentioned before, can you listen to music while you work? Can you break the task up into small enough chunks that you can enjoy doing them? Can you trade tasks with others in your group so you all focus on what you enjoy and do well?

We've all heard about people who say they are excited to get up in the morning and get to work. The reason they are able to do this is because they have enthusiasm for what they do. Find it for yourself, and you won't regret it.

Be Childlike

Being childlike is more than just playing. Think about a child in your life. No, not the annoying one that you can't stand seeing because he's a brat! Think about the one you like who smiles and laughs. What qualities does he have?

For one, he's probably very curious. When a child sees and hears something new for the first time, he is absolutely enamored. He also probably finds himself laughing for no reason. You would do well do adopt a sense of curiosity. Consider how all those things in your life that you don't like or are afraid to do or try would change if you became curious about them.

Children are also persistent when they care about what it is they are doing. Persistence will be covered in the next chapter, but think about how a child can act when she really wants something! It's not just when she holds her breath until you buy her ice cream – it can also be when she is engrossed trying to figure something out. She will keep poking and prodding until she gets it.

Children also like to get involved. Until society makes them self-conscious and shy, children like to jump in, help out, talk to others, etc. They don't sit on the sidelines – they get in the game! What a wonderful quality to adopt. It's the people who get involved who have the fun and get the success. Most people convince themselves that they just like to sit and watch. But really that idea comes from fear, or from an inner resistance that has convinced them to "sit out." Everyone's idea of getting involved is different. There are definitely times I beg off of doing something, or stay in and read instead of going out. But if you always sit on the sidelines, chances are you are missing out on a lot of things.

What's amazing is how obvious this becomes when watching people improvise. When I have new improvisers act out a scene, they invariably "resist" each other's offers. For example, if two people are acting out being a married couple and the man says, "Honey, let's go out dancing tonight," ninety percent of the time an inexperienced improviser will resist that action and say something like, "Oh, I don't feel like it."

The thing is that when you improvise on stage, your first instincts come out. Most people react that way (resisting) in an improv scene because that's the easiest course of action! Even though it's just an improv scene, it's safer to take no action than to say, "yes" (this will be covered in much greater detail in the section on "yes and").

What does this mean in the real world? At work, do you take on new projects, or committees? Do you help out in activities? At home, do you take part in your family's activities as a volunteer or chaperone? In your community or with any associations you join, do you just show up at events or do you get involved on committees or in leadership?

Getting involved doesn't mean you have to become president of every group you join. But you only ever get out what you put in, and that goes for just about everything in life. Kids are born with this knowledge, and then forget it as they grow up...

There is an important distinction to make here. Being "childlike" is good; being "childish" is bad!

To be childish means to be selfish, petulant, irresponsible, and petty. Many, many adults have no problem being childish!

To be childlike is to be curious and persistent. It means to get involved. You probably did these things as a child, so get them back and you will naturally have more fun in your life.

Laugh More

Laugh. Laugh often and laugh hard.

Laugh everyday. Laugh multiple times a day.

What should you laugh at? That's up to you. There's no "universal funny." I can't tell you what to do to laugh. Find out for yourself, and do it. Do it often. For me it's watching funny movies and TV shows and talking with friends who make me laugh. I also listen to the same hilarious radio show in Philadelphia every morning. For you it may be one of these, but it may not. You may like to read funny books and articles, or maybe people watching makes you laugh. What you do to laugh isn't important, as long as you are doing something.

Even better than doing things that make you life is to see the humor in everyday situations. There is funny stuff out there, you just have to look for it. Once you simply start to pay attention to the world around you with the focus of, "what's funny about this?" you will realize how absurd the world is. Without even trying you will find yourself laughing and smiling.

When you laugh, your body releases positive chemicals into your system. Laughing reduces your stress, increases your blood flow, improves the immune system, improves your mood, and can even be used to reduce pain and cure disease.

The more laugh, the healthier you will be and the more able you will be to handle all of the unpredictable twists life throws your way.

Remember, to get free access to over 25 exercises and improv games to help practice these principles, visit www.AvishParashar.com/bookbonus

Have Fun!

Principle #2:

It's All In Your Head

After an improv comedy performance, I commonly hear the comment, "Oh, I could never do that." Even when I try to explain to the person that it's just a matter of practice and training, they will often come back to me saying, "Some people are just born with that ability."

The first thing that jumps into my mind in these situations is that a person who has never done improv is telling me, an experienced performer and teacher of improv, whether learning improv is possible! This is really not that surprising. It is easy to sit back and watch if you think that some people are just born with talent and it's ok for you to be unable to do it yourself. But if someone comes along and tells you that anyone, even you, can do it with the right training and experience, then suddenly you almost feel flawed. You question, "If anyone can do this, why can't I?"

This is, of course, fallacious thinking. You don't criticize a 3-month-old baby for not knowing how to walk, do you? You don't criticize a 16-year-old who's behind the wheel of a car for the first time for not being able to drive properly, right? In the same way, there is no shame in not knowing how to improvise *right now*. You've never been trained to do it properly.

There is great shame, however, in looking at something and refusing to believe it is possible for you to do it. You may decide that you don't want to do it, or that it's not worth doing. You may determine your priorities are elsewhere. Barring those few exceptions where a physical limitation gets in the way, you must acknowledge that you can do it, if that is what you want. For example, I may love basketball, but at my age and height (5'7") being a basketball star is not likely to happen (although shorter players than I have made it).

Most people don't succumb to physical limitations; they succumb to mental limitations.

Could you be a famous concert pianist, even if you have never played the piano? Unless you are tone deaf, the answer is yes. You would likely have to sacrifice every other area of your life to practice 8 hours a day and start touring the world performing. To most people, this cost would be too high. Again, there is no shame in making that choice. The question is, how many people do you know (maybe yourself included) have left dreams by the wayside not because the cost was too high, but because they decided they just couldn't come true? They didn't bother trying or starting something new or different because they believed it to be too late, too much, or just plain impossible.

There are a few mentalities that lead to great improvisation. When applied, they open you up to a whole new world of possibilities.

Technique vs. Mentality

Whenever I teach anything, be it improv, martial arts, communication, sales, or whatever, I always start with mentality. This often causes a slight problem because what people are looking for is technique.

For example, in improv comedy there are hundreds of games, many of which are described in this book. Often, whether in rehearsals with my own group or when I was teaching a class, people were eager to learn new games. We would work on one idea or game for a session or two, and people started to feel the urge to learn something new. At times, in fact, they became bored with repeating the same game. This is not to say that they mastered the games they knew already. That was far from the reality. Once they had gained familiarity with a game, they felt they were ready for something different.

This is not a slight against any of my former students. It is a very natural tendency in this over-stimulated, MTV world. We are all constantly seeking the next interesting thing. In any endeavor, however, the greatest impact does not come from learning more and more and newer and newer techniques. Greatness comes from practicing the fundamentals over and over again until they are completely second nature.

In sports, the fundamentals are physical and must be repeatedly practiced (shooting free throws, serving a tennis ball, etc). In music, fundamentals come in the form of practicing scales and drilling with fingering exercises.

In improvisation, the fundamentals are mental. While the creative space of the improviser is a stage, the world of the improviser is in his thought processes. Everything the improviser does begins in his head. As such, the best way to build a strong improviser is to train the underlying mentality rather than teaching him a variety of skills or games (In fact, most improvisers I have seen with heavy "skills" training from day 1 often have

"Greatness comes from practicing the fundamentals over and over again until they are completely second nature"

a cap on their potential because they have never built the underlying mindset of great improv).

In the same way, whether professionally or personally, everything you do in your world begins in your head. To increase your effectiveness and success, seek first to adopt the key mentalities of achievement. For example, I conducted sales training where I interviewed attendees in advance to find out what were their challenges on the job and their expectations of the training. Sure enough, quite a few hoped to learn "a few new closing or opening techniques." During the session we worked on mentality and fundamentals instead, and the results were quite positive.

Why This is Important

Techniques are wonderful and needed, but only after the mindsets have been trained. They are like tools. They are incredibly useful, but relying just on those tools will not develop the underlying skills you need to deal with an unfamiliar situation when it arises. For example, if you know how to use a wrench, screwdriver, and hammer, you will be fine doing basic projects. But if those are your only tools, and a situation arises where pliers would be useful, you will have no idea what to do. In fact, you might try to force one of the other tools to work, which is a recipe for disaster.

If, however, you have an underlying knowledge of construction, you will be able to understand what needs to be done even if you aren't currently familiar with the tool. Rather than forcing an existing tool, you can look for something different and appropriate, or invent something new (indeed, this is how most progress originates).

Once you have an underlying mindset, you have freedom and flexibility to deal with any situation, not just the specific ones you for which you have prepared. The challenge is that it can be a longer and harder road to train a mindset than a technique, especially in the beginning. This goes back to the question at the beginning of the chapter. If someone says, "I could never do that," the first half of the response is, "Anyone can do that, it's just a matter of training and experience." The second half of the response (usually left unsaid) is, "Most people are just unwilling to develop the mindset to be able to do great improv."

This applies to any area of your life. If you want to be great at something, learn and adopt the underlying mentalities that make success easy, natural, and inevitable.

Key Mentalities

Here are the key mentalities that lead not only to great improv, but also to success in many other areas.

Willingness

The key to success in any area of life, improv or otherwise, is to be *willing*. Willing to do what? You must be willing to do many things, actually.

Willingness to Fail

First, you have to be willing to fail. In improv comedy, you never know what's going to happen on the stage. Sometimes an audience is just not with you (or worse, they're drunk!). Sometimes an audience will throw you a curveball that for whatever reason knocks you off balance. Sometimes you don't connect with them, and sometimes you say and do stuff that isn't that funny. As a performer, you have to accept that these things will happen. You have to be willing to mess it up big time.

Life is the same way. Some days the wind just doesn't blow our way. Sometimes we won't connect with people, or we'll mess up the interaction. Sometimes we will try our darndest and still come up short.

Again, you have to be willing to fail. The important distinction is that being willing to fail does not mean that you want to fail. In fact, you must want and intend to succeed. Acknowledging that you may fail just means you will not be paralyzed by fear. You won't avoid taking action because of thoughts like, "But what if I fail?!" One of life's great ironies is that the more willing you are to do so, the less likely you are to actually fail! Once you accept the possibility of failure, it loses it's hold over you. This lets you focus on doing the task at hand.

Imagine that you are an improv performer, and you are about to take the stage for the first time. For most people, this creates a sense of nerves and fear. If you put your attention on what frightens you, then you have less attention to put on the skills you have learned, on the audience, and on the performance itself. You have already reduced the likelihood that you will succeed before you have even taken the stage.

Another great irony is that in order to succeed, you must fail!

For years, I had the good fortune of getting a part at every single audition I attended. From high-school through college, and for a year or so afterwards, I never "failed" at an audition. By eight years after college, I only once was I not chosen for a part! I was pretty proud of myself. I thought that I must be pretty amazing to always get cast. Unfortunately, I was deluding myself. No one succeeds all the time. If you never fail, than you are simply not doing enough! I kept getting parts because I kept

"If you have no failures at all, then maybe you should consider doing more."

going to auditions where I knew I was eminently qualified for the role. I knew my chance of success was very high. This is the acting equivalent of playing it safe. Yes, I played many parts, but I would never progress in my life or career by playing it safe.

Keep track of your failures. As long as you learn from them (and don't do anything stupid to burn bridges or hurt yourself!) they will be indicators that you are on the road to success.

I hope you end up with more success than failures. But, if you have no failures at all, then maybe you should consider doing more.

Willingness to Look Foolish

This could also be classified as the fear of embarrassment. As an improv performer, I have portrayed dogs, bears, gorillas, and a multitude of other animals. I have taken on accents and imitated celebrities that were very far off from reality. I have sung at the top of my lungs, usually off key. The wild and crazy world of improv comedy requires you to be silly and look foolish. You absolutely can not perform improv effectively if you are afraid of looking silly (although I have seen people try; it's not pretty...).

Chances are that you will never have to act like an animal in front of your colleagues or loved ones. However, if you are not willing to look foolish, you will not only reduce your chance of success, you will also miss out on some wonderful opportunities.

Think back in your life. Have you ever kept silent or chosen not to ask a question because you were afraid of looking ignorant? If so, have you ever had the experience where someone else spoke up and said the same thing you were going to, and it was well received?

Can you think back on an opportunity on which you missed out because you were afraid of looking foolish? Perhaps you didn't apply for a job, skipped an audition or tryout, or missed advice because you didn't ask for it. Has there been a man or woman you didn't approach or ask out on a date because you were afraid of how you would look? I won't insult you by pointing out how foolish it is to afraid to look foolish, mostly because it is common and universal (and I suffer from that fear just like everyone else).

Remember this though: People are generally not afraid of *being foolish*, but rather of *looking foolish*. I suggest you ask yourself this, "To whom do I care about looking foolish?" Quite often, the answer is, "people I don't know or care about."

We don't do things that would better or enrich our lives because we are afraid of what people whom we don't know might think! How crazy is that??

Every time you make the choice not to take action because you are afraid of looking foolish, just remind yourself that you are letting other people determine the quality of life you will enjoy. You are putting more stock in their opinions of you than in what you want to do or achieve. Besides, half of the time you will be wrong, and they won't think you're foolish at all. In fact, many will admire your action. The rest won't think twice about you. Remember, "you wouldn't care what people thought of you if you realized how seldom they do."

Willingness to Be Rejected

Ah rejection…is there anything out there that we try to avoid more?

The fear of rejection comes from our desire to connect and belong. If someone rejects us, then maybe we have done something wrong. Rejection goes hand in hand with embarrassment. Often it isn't hearing the "no" that bothers us. We automatically associate the "no" with rejection and that causes us to feel embarrassment.

It's okay to not like rejection. You just can not be paralyzed by it. The problem is two-fold. First, in order to succeed you **must** face lots of rejection and learn how to deal with it in a positive way. Second, the more successful you become, the more rejection you will face! Because of this, many people choose to settle in their lives. If you don't understand how to positively deal with rejection, then of course you are going to avoid putting yourself in a position to be rejected. But the reality is that in order to really succeed at anything you choose to do, you must face rejection.

When I first started my own business (soon after college), I was speaking to a friend's father about how much I hated cold-calling. He looked at me and said, "That's because you have never failed in school. You've always gotten good grades and succeeded. The person who's got the edge is the guy who failed a class and learned that he could get back up and still do well."

At the time, that conversation struck me as strange. Here was someone telling me that having been successful in school was a limitation! I soon realized that he was right. Not that I think getting good grades was a bad thing, but rather, that having avoided major failure and rejection in my life, I had not built up a resistance to it. As his words sank in, I realized that I needed to overcome that fear.

Soon, after having made over 600 cold calls, I can't say that I enjoyed rejection, but I did get to a point where I no longer let it rule me.

Willingness to Be Wrong

Nobody likes to be wrong. In fact, from the day we start moving around and walking and talking, we are constantly being told what's right and wrong.

It starts at home, with parents consistently reminding us of what we can and can not do. Then we go off to school and the teachers pick up where our parents left off with regard to behavior, plus we are introduced to the concept of grades. From this point on, everything we do will be evaluated. And most of it will be presented with a sense of black and white – no gray areas between right and wrong..

For years and years we struggle and work to come up with the right answer, whether it's for a test, essay, report, or oral answer. It's no wonder that once people reach adulthood, they fear being wrong. We are so conditioned to find the right answer that we are always fearing penalties for being wrong. And yet, just like in our approach to failure, we have to be willing to be wrong to move forward in our lives. The only things we will know with 100% certainty are the things we already know well. I believe you will be hard pressed to move forward in your life and progress if you stay wrapped up just within what you know.

Being wrong may often be a precursor to failure. If you have an idea for a product you assume the world will love and you invest in it and are wrong, well, now you have a failure on your hands. As with all the other states of willingness, the point is not that there are no consequences to being wrong, Rather, you must accept that sometimes you *will* be wrong. In fact, being wrong, and learning from it, is how you grow. The reality is that most people learn from making mistakes faster than they do by being right.

When directing new improvisers, I have found that some people came in with natural instincts that allowed them to make good improv choices right off the bat (choices we will discuss throughout this book). Others, however, needed much "feedback" to learn how to do it.

Looking back, the people who became the strongest performers weren't the ones who came in with the most natural talent. The people who became very strong were the ones who were willing to learn.

The people without natural talent who were willing to get out there and try, without fear of being wrong, were able to take correction and incorporate the lessons into their performances. They became very good very quickly, because they were willing to be wrong and learn from it. At times, some of the people with natural talent were the hardest to train because they had been doing things a certain way for so long and they found it very hard to let go of that to try things in a new and better way.

Remember, it's not being wrong that's the problem; it's not doing the right things when you are wrong to move forward. What are the right things? I'm glad you asked...

1) Admit It

There is nothing more annoying than a person who is wrong and will not admit it. You've probably seen the type: the guy who acts super-confident, turns out to be wrong, and then rather than saying, "Oh hey, I was wrong," he (or she – ladies are just as susceptible to this!) either moves on without acknowledging the error or blames it on something outside of himself.

Admitting being wrong is often perceived as a sign of weakness or lower intelligence (and understandably, since when we were growing up, being wrong dropped our grade a notch or two...). I have found though, that admitting error is a sign of tremendous strength and character. If you don't admit you are wrong, you can not learn and grow.

It takes a confident person to admit when he is wrong. If you admit a mistake you are saying to the world that you understand that you are human, and that you have the character to admit and it fix it. (This does depend a bit on your delivery – some people admit they are wrong so often and so meekly that they are betraying their lack of confidence. Don't admit to being wrong if you clearly aren't, and don't lower your status – we'll cover status a but later – when you admit it.)

Admitting when you are wrong has long term benefits too. If you regularly interact with a group of people and never admit it when you are wrong, your credibility drops. In any disagreement, they will put less stock in what you say because you have a history of arguing strongly whether you are right or not. If, however, you admit to being wrong on occasion, then people will actually respect your ideas more. When you strongly defend a point, it will give them pause because they know that if you are pushing hard, you must really believe in what you are saying.

2) Learn From Your Errors

There is a famous saying, "Fool me once, shame on you. Fool me twice, shame on me." Quite simply, this means that it's okay to make a mistake, but if you make it twice, than there's something wrong.

It's okay to be wrong, but if you are repeatedly wrong about the same thing, then you are not learning from your mistake, and you are doomed to forever repeat the error until you get a clue!

Here's a story of what an idiot I can be when it comes to this stuff.

I hate taking my car into the garage to get stuff checked out. I don't know much about cars and car repair, I don't like to take the time out of my day (and be without a car) and I'm always afraid that I will get fleeced by someone who knows how little I know. For a little while my car was a little slow starting. On occasion, the engine would take 1-3 seconds to turn over. I knew this could be due to a few things, so I held off getting it checked out.

One day, I found myself sitting in my garage in a car that wouldn't start. I turned the key and nothing happened. I was persistent, waited a few minutes and tried again, it worked!

This is a "fool me once, shame on you moment." The clear sign here was for me to get the car checked out. But did I? No, of course not! Why? Because the next couple of times the car started fine.

I know you can see where this is going. A week or two later, I hopped into my car that was parked on a street in North Philadelphia. I turned the key, and nothing happened. This time however, all of my retries netted nothing. I had to call a tow truck and wait in my car for an hour until the truck took me to a garage. One thing I can tell you for sure. I will not be letting "little problems" with my car go on for that long again.

This is a clear example of how we set ourselves up for bigger problems when we don't learn from our errors and take action. If you are wrong about facts or make an error in judgment, admit it, then learn from it and don't do it again!

Willingness to Do What it Takes to Grow

So far, we have seen that being willing to fail, make mistakes, be rejected, and be wrong all can lead to personal growth. What's amazing to me is that some people are even unwilling to grow at all!

It took me a while to recognize and accept this fact about people. I am a person who feels it is important to continually grow and improve oneself, so it was unbelievable to me that some people would choose the opposite. What I discovered though is that some people really fear the change and uncertainty of growth.

For people who are comfortable and set in their ways, this is not so unbelievable. Why risk the potential upheaval of life changes if everything is hunky-dory as is?

In looking back on my own life, I realize that this is not so unbelievable at all. In my early days, when I had huge dreams but limited success, I would occasionally lament that it would be better not to try than to try and fail. If a person never tries, he could tell stories forever such as, "Oh yeah, I used to do improv comedy. I probably could have done it professionally, but I just got busy and gave it up." If he tried and failed, he would forever believe that he could not have done it.

I honestly think that this is what keeps many people from trying. Why rock the boat? You can always sit around the bar telling tales of the "glory days." But, when you take a long, realistic look at this, you quickly realize that is a crazy way to live – and a sure fire way to short change yourself of the quality of life you deserve. By not trying you preserve the dream – but that's all it will ever be - a dream. Deep down, you will always regret not going for it.

In addition to failure, rejection, and embarrassment, when you put yourself out there to learn and grow you also open yourself up to uncertainty.

Imagine that you work an ordinary 9 to 5 job. Let's say you go back to grad school to get an advanced degree. When you finish, you would most likely change jobs, or at least positions. For some people this is scary, especially it is an enjoyable 9 to 5 job.

One of the harder things I've done was to leave a job I really liked to start an internet company. I left stability, comfort, and people with whom I loved to work, for uncertainty. Many people leave jobs to start companies because they don't like their current situation. I actually loved my situation. I left only because I knew that if I was still there five years later, it would have meant I had not done the things I set out to achieve in my life.

And you know what? The internet company failed! Failed big time! Then I went full time into improv comedy – and that failed! But that led me to my current career – professional speaking and information marketing. I still use the improv, I get to perform, and I get to help people (while getting paid to do it!). I love what I do now, but it took stepping forward, taking risks, learning and growing, and a fair amount of failure to get here.

Seek out opportunities to grow. If you pass up an opportunity, make sure it is because you really don't want it, or that it really won't serve you in the long run. Don't let fear stop you from doing what you want to do.

Be willing – you won't be sorry.

Believe in Yourself

At the core of improvisation is your own belief in your ability to do it. Nothing else matters, in improvisation or any other area of life.

Some improv games are more challenging than others. On occasion, when I announce to a group in rehearsal that we will be working on a more difficult game, I hear groans or complaints from the group. While this can be done in good fun, it often belies an underlying dread of playing a difficult game.

So, I will often put in a "no-complaining" rule. That is, if I am going to have people do something challenging, I will forbid people from groaning or saying, "Oh no!" This is not just to create a positive atmosphere (though that is nice). If you convince yourself that something is hard, it will be.

I'm sure you can relate to the following story that illustrates this concept.

Now and then I will run for exercise. I'm not a super big fan of running, but I realize that from a cardiovascular standpoint it's incredibly beneficial. I don't go very fast, but I like to go for at least 20 minutes. I also happen to find myself really pushing and struggling if I run much longer than 30 minutes. .

One day I was on a treadmill and I was running along, listening to music. I throw a towel over the display so I can't keep looking at

"Don't let fear stop you from doing what you want to do."

the time (a practice which makes time seemingly stop!). I was doing vague calculations in my head based on how long I thought the songs were and how many songs had gone by. I noticed that it was getting a little tough, but I knew I was under 30 minutes so I kept going. No big deal. When the final song finished, I slowed down and removed the towel. To my surprise, I had been running for 45 minutes! It turns out I had miscalculated – I underestimated how long how each song was, and I also forgot about two of the songs on my play list.

Here's the point – while I assumed that I was still running within my capabilities (under 30 minutes), I felt fine. Had I been looking at the clock, once the 30-minute mark passed I would have quickly felt tired and drained ("I can't go on!").

I'm sure you can think of a time in your life when you achieved far more than you thought possible because you mistakenly thought something was easier than you otherwise would have. And as result, because of your belief, it was! This is why I don't like improvisers complaining about difficult exercises. They are setting themselves up for failure.

In the same way, you should not focus on how difficult or impossible something is. Rather, adopt the belief that you can do it, no matter what.

This is doubly true for things that you have to do, but don't want to do. Take public speaking, for instance. Many, many people dread public speaking. Yet, many of these people often have to get up and speak in front of others for work or other presentations. The worst thing people can do is to think about how awful it is going to be and how, "I can't do this!" And yet, that's exactly the thought process that most people go through.

As clichéd as it is, you have to believe in yourself. Think about the little engine that could ("I think I can...").

This doesn't mean that you lie to yourself. If you have never spoken in public and are terrified of it, you don't have to say to yourself, "I am going to do the best speech anyone has ever seen." If you can say that and believe, that's great, but you would be better off saying, "I know I can do this and do a good job," in a way that you can believe.

The important thing is that you believe in yourself. The more you believe in your abilities, the better you will do.

Have Commitment

Commitment is a strange concept when you think about improv comedy, because it seems like very little commitment is required. Once the improvised scene is done (anywhere from 1-20 minutes) the scene is gone forever – where's the commitment?

Commitment in improvisation is about commitment in the moment. When a performer takes the stage, she must be 100% committed to what she is doing. This is the only way to be successful in improv.

I have seen many performers take the stage and begin acting out a character. But it was clear that they had doubts about their character choice (maybe they thought it was too goofy, or out there, or weird, or they were unsure about their acting ability). No matter how funny or good their words were, something about the performance just didn't connect.

In improv, when a performer chooses a character, she must throw herself into it 100%. In an improvised game, she must be 100% there. When she isn't, the audience can tell and the work suffers.

A clear way to observe this is to watch new and experienced dancers. While there will be a difference in their movements and grace, one of the most obvious differences is in the commitment. A new dancer looks a little hesitant, as if she is holding back. Experienced dancers, while performing, look almost lost in their performances. That's 100% being there. That's commitment.

This mentality is a vital principle of success in any endeavor. Most people go through their lives, personal and professional, without any real sense of commitment. While at work, their minds are on their personal lives. While at home, their minds are on what they have to do at work. When trying something new, they hedge their bets and never fully try.

This is not to be confused with "getting your ducks in a row." Hedging your bets means never throwing yourself 100% into a task. This way, if you fail you can say, "Well, I didn't try my hardest." It also creates a false sense of security. Getting your ducks in a row just means that you set your life up so that if you fail, it won't be the end of the world. Getting your ducks in a row actually allows you to commit 100% because you know that no matter what happens, you will be okay.

Think about the things in your life that are not where you want them to be. Chances are you have not committed 100% to them. Yes, in many areas, you can "half-ass" it and do well enough. But in the important areas of your life (family, work, dreams, health, etc) you should never settle for "ok." Commit now to adopting this mentality and getting all you deserve.

Have Persistence

In the fast-paced, quickly-changing world of improvisational comedy, talking about persistence may sound very odd. Improv is described as "disposable theater," (as soon as a game is done, it's gone) so what does that have to do with persistence? Actually, it has a few very real things to do with it.

First, 99% of the people who begin doing improv start under the wrong assumption. They believe that improv is about being quick-witted and funny, and making jokes. Improv is not about these things, so almost everyone who learns improv has to have the persistence to drill and drill to retrain their minds to think improvisationally.

Second, from a performance standpoint, many people get the idea of "one-shot-homerun" in their heads. They believe that they need to start out with a great idea in order to create a great improv scene or game. This is not the case at all, but the performer needs the persistence to continue on with an idea that seems very basic.

Oftentimes in an improv game, an idea is introduced that doesn't get the best response from the crowd. An inexperienced (or just bad) performer may panic and throw that idea away or introduce something completely new in hopes of improving things. This invariably creates confusion both on stage and with the audience. It creates a disjointed game that doesn't make anybody happy.

The experienced performer realizes that with a little persistence and "sticktoitiveness" those offers can often lead to brilliant performance. It's only a matter of pushing through, trusting the process, and doing what he knows is right. When the performer does this, the result is usually a very solid game.

In life and in business, people are too often willing to throw in the towel when things don't work. Or they don't really get started until everything is right in place and the path is totally clear. The path will never be totally clear, and things won't always work. The key is to persist in the face of these things, trust your process (whatever it may be) and do what you know to be right. The result will usually be something wonderful.

The Flip Side

One caveat does need to be stated here: in life, as in improv, there is a difference between being persistent and being foolhardy. I have seen improv scenes go on far longer than they should because the performers refuse to let go and move on. Sometimes mercy killing is a good thing!

The same rule applies in life. Sometimes you have to let go and move on, whether it's regarding a job, a relationship, or even a dream.

When I ran my own improv group, it was my dream. I wanted to make the group huge and successful and world famous. Six years later, I decided it was time to close the doors and move on to other things. Was this because the group was failing financially or in any way? No, we were doing well. I just realized that the group had changed, my life had changed, and it was time to let go and move on. In retrospect, that decision could have been made earlier, but it usually takes longer than we'd like for realizations like that to sink in.

The nice benefit to letting go was that I discovered things that fulfill me even more than the improv group was. Sometimes you have to make space for new stuff to show up.

So how can you know whether you are being persistent or foolhardy? It's not always easy. The answer is to trust and listen to yourself. Persistence is when you know deep down that you are doing the right thing for you and those around you. Foolhardy is when your ego is telling you not to give up because you will be a failure. Persistence is intelligent, foolhardy is stubborn.

The only way to make this distinction is to really be honest with yourself. Are you at a job that you don't enjoy because you honestly believe that it will get better once the "busy season" ends like everyone says? Or are you hanging in there because you don't want to look for another job? Are you staying with someone because you honestly deep down believe you are right for each other, or because you have a belief that you have to stick it out to be a good person (hint: if you're having these thoughts, that's a sign that the second is probably true!)

Understand the difference, and make to sure to persist in the things that are vitally important to you and that you know are right, and let the other stuff go.

Discipline

Discipline goes hand in hand with persistence. In improv, and in any other performance, there is the idea of the "creative genius." This is the idea that some people are just born with talent and can do things naturally. While there is something to be said for natural gifts, what most people don't realize is that behind the effortless ease and genius lies years and years of discipline and hard work.

The musical virtuoso may have had a natural gift for music, but chances are she sat at her piano for many hours practicing everyday. Great authors write and write and write, often writing volumes before their first success. Natural gifts only take you so far. After that, it's discipline that makes the difference.

Some people have natural gifts to which they don't apply discipline. They are called *hobbyists*. They are the "natural" cooks, handymen, knitters, storytellers, and speakers, etc. There is nothing wrong with this. All of us need to prioritize our lives and decide where to put our energy. The point is to make sure that you don't delude yourself into thinking that the people who make it get by on just their natural talent.

On the other hand, people without "natural" talent can often make it by applying discipline. Hard work and consistent practice can lead to great things.

I have seen it many times while teaching improv. People with no special starting skill but with the right mindset of learning, improving, and working will always become solid, if not great, improvisers. By the same token, I have seen people who have a great deal of inherent talent, but no discipline, only go so far because they were unwilling to work at it.

"Behind the effortless ease and genius lies years and years of discipline and hard work."

This idea does not just apply to creative endeavors. Natural sales people have probably been selling their whole lives, even if they didn't know they were doing it. Great computer programmers have written thousands and thousands of lines of code. We all know that in the medical profession Residents work consistent 80-hour weeks developing their skills.

There is no substitute for consistency and discipline. With discipline, untalented people can make great strides. But without discipline, even the most talented person can only achieve so much.

If you were to stop reading this and do nothing but apply the mentalities in this chapter, I guarantee you that you would see magnificent changes in your life. I hope you continue reading, but as you do, keep in mind that every upcoming lesson comes from the same place - having the right mentality.

Remember, to get free access to over 25 exercises and improv games to help practice these principles, visit **www.AvishParashar.com/bookbonus**

Principle #3:

Express Yourself

Ultimately, improv comedy, or at least good improv comedy, is about self-expression. That is, the best improv happens not when the performers are trying to be funny, but rather when they are being themselves on stage. The performers can feel it, audiences can see it, and the end result is great improvisation.

Improv comedy is an interesting thing. As a performer, you take the stage with nothing prepared – no script, no outline, no nothing. Then, based on an audience suggestion (or sometimes not) you create comedy and theater on the spot.

This dynamic is both extremely rewarding and makes the performer extremely vulnerable. When you succeed, you can truly credit yourself because you, along with your scene partners, created something that worked well. The vulnerability comes due to the fact that when you don't do well, there's not a whole lot of other people to blame. There is no director or writer. Sure you can point a finger at the other improvisers, but in addition to making you a bad team player, that also is a bit of avoidance.

In improv, you are responsible for your own success and failure.

What's even harder about improv is that since you are making it all up in the moment, what you reveal on stage is what's inside of you at that moment. Improvisers, especially new ones, feel immense fear at this prospect because they are essentially baring their souls to the audience.

If I am doing a scene and I swear, or make an offensive comment, or act like a mean old cuss, even if it's in character, there is a fear that the audience will judge me for it. As a result, improvisers have a natural reaction to put up a wall between themselves and their art. That is, rather than expressing themselves naturally on stage they tend to filter everything they do to make sure it's "ok." The result of this is an improv performance that is not very engaging to watch.

A second defense mechanism is to try to emulate successful improvisers. A new person will see what an experienced performer does, and rather than just be himself, he tries to perform like the veteran. On the surface, this seems like a sound strategy because if a talented performer is doing something, it must be right. It also serves as a way to "protect" the improviser because if you are not really being yourself and you do something wrong, well, it's not you!

However, the only thing that makes improv worth watching and performing is the idea of self-expression. When a performer takes the stage, he must be willing to be 100% himself and go with his instincts (in a character choice sense – new improvisers need to retrain many instincts when it comes to skills!) Time and again, the best performers I have seen do this. Also, the performers I have seen advance the fastest embrace this idea very early on.

This is true not just for improvisation, but in any art form. It is the most evident in improv comedy because, as I said, you are creating content on the spot and role playing. But any accomplished musician, dancer, artists, writer will tell you that what makes his work special is that he expresses himself through his art.

Why This is Important

I know the concept of the artists "expressing themselves through his art" is a bit clichéd. The saying conjures up an image of a recluse who has no social skills and spends twenty hours a day on his artwork. He is misunderstood, will not be appreciated until after his time...

This does not have to be the case at all. Self-expression does not preclude social skill!

That stereotype comes from two places:

1) Disapproval

In order to fully express yourself, you have to be willing to do it in the face of disapproval. While no one cares what *everyone* thinks, most of us care what *most* people think. As such, we are reluctant to express our true selves for fear of disapproval. The reclusive artist long ago abandoned the need for this kind of approval.

Of course, not caring what others think doesn't mean you have to intentionally put them off. The world is about balance, and there are many people who express themselves through their art (or work – we'll see how in a minute!) who don't alienate the rest of the world. My advice – fall into this category – the world is too interesting and has too many interesting and rewarding people and things for you to be a recluse!

2) Lack of Ability

If the only way to express yourself is through your art, then you never developed the skill to express yourself in other ways, such as conversation and basic human interaction. This is why the stereotype of the "tortured artist" exists. People with a rough childhood generally do not develop the ability to communicate and express themselves properly, so they turn to art. (**This doesn't mean that this is the only way**) To be in balance, you should have both – the ability to express yourself and the ability to interact with others

What does all this art talk have to do with you? Self-expression is not limited to just art. The ability to express yourself is a key success principle in anything you do.

In a previous chapter, I wrote about having enthusiasm and passion. Where does that enthusiasm and passion come from? From self-expression, of course! There is the person you are, deep down inside. You have dreams, ideas, visions, likes, dislikes, etc. The greatest cause for dissatisfaction is when you ignore that, push it aside, or just don't feed it. When you are not expressing who you are, you are cutting yourself off from who you want and are meant to be.

"When you are not expressing who you are, you are cutting yourself off from who you want and are meant to be."

I firmly believe this is what leads to the dreaded "mid-life crisis." People spend years ignoring this part of them, doing what they feel they "have to," being a "responsible adult." But, like a dam trying to hold back a river that keeps increasing the pressure, eventually the real self bursts out.

What's sad is that it happens so much later in life ("mid-life") when it is much harder and after so much time is past. What's even sadder is that some people are in such strong denial that they never let the dam burst. They live their entire lives never experiencing the joy of who they want and are meant to be...

This is the Key to Satisfaction and Fulfillment

Everyone is looking for satisfaction and fulfillment. While everyone would love to have a lot of money, most people would prefer to have enough money to be comfortable and satisfied instead of having gobs of money and being unsatisfied.

The challenge many, many people face is that they don't know what they want! I have had numerous conversations with people who know that they don't want to be doing for the rest of their lives what they are currently doing. But, when asked, "What do you want to do?" they can provide no answer. Some mumble something vague, ("I don't know, something outdoors."), some evade the question, and some get downright uncomfortable or annoyed.

The answer to that questions starts with self-expression. When you are able to be yourself 100%, fulfillment follows.

The important thing here is that self-expression is a process, not a switch! You don't one day suddenly decide, "Okay, now I am going to express myself!" Okay, actually you do, but that doesn't mean that it happens in an instant.

Making the decision is a critical first step, but the only way to really embrace this idea is to constantly remind yourself to do it. You must also practice and develop your abilities so that you can really express yourself by uncovering layers to get to your inner person..

Be Courageous

The first step in the process is to be courageous. Many people put off this process because it is scary. You may have been ignoring what's inside of you for so long that you are afraid of what might come out.

I once tried to get a friend to do this process. She knew she was unhappy in what she was doing, but she didn't know what to do about it. I suggested some techniques covered later in this chapter to help her figure some things out, but she was incredibly resistant. When I pushed her on why, she said because she was afraid of what would come out.

I have to admit, I was a little stunned. This was the first time I encountered a situation where a person resisted doing something because she was afraid of learning about herself! And yet, from that point on, as I watched people and saw how they went about living their lives, that attitude seemed to make sense.

People spend a tremendous amount of time learning about others, watching other people, and *judging other people.* They spend almost no time learning about themselves. This level of avoidance comes from fear; fear of self-discovery; fear of what you might learn about yourself; fear of facing truths that you would rather not face. Unfortunately, the path to real fulfillment and success lies on the other side of that fear. Without tapping deep inside of yourself, how can you ever know what will truly make you happy?

Peel Away the layers

Think of yourself as an onion. You have layers. If you have spent years not really learning about yourself, then you will have many, many layers. This means that you will need to take some time to peel away those layers and dig deep.

To do this, you will need commitment to the process. You can not expect to sit down and do an exercise once and suddenly say, "Hey, I'm expressing myself!" Over time, you will learn a little more and a little more. Sometimes you will think you've stumbled upon something really big, only to discover later that the big thing was just one more layer above the *really* big thing!

Journaling, Meditating

Three simple non-improv comedy ways of peeling away the layers are meditation, silence and journaling.

When you meditate, you sit in silence and empty your mind of thought. You can do this by focusing on your breathing, gently pushing thoughts away, or repeating a phrase or mantra. This is not a meditation guide (there are hundreds of books on the topic, or just type "meditation" into Google), but if you want to try this, sit on the floor or in a comfortable chair, close your eyes, and breathe deeply in and out. Focus on your breathing. As thoughts arise, don't fight them, but rather acknowledge them, let them go, and focus back in on your breathing. This sounds simple, but if you have never done it before you may find yourself struggling to keep at it for more than 5 minutes! Don't struggle, just do it consistently for as long as it is comfortable. You will find it getting easier and easier.

Silence is like meditation, only you don't force yourself to not think. You can do this sitting in a chair or on the floor. Just be in silence – no conversation, no TV or radio, no distractions of any sort. As thoughts come up, feel free to let them. The longer you sit in silence, the more you may be amazed by what comes up from inside of you.

You don't have to do this sitting. You can go outside and walk while you do this. The key however is to be without distraction, so walking down a busy street with lots of people and cars is not the best bet. If you can walk in a peaceful natural environment, that can work quite well.

When you journal, you simply write in a stream of consciousness fashion. Simply take a few pieces of paper and start writing. It doesn't matter what you write, as long as you keep your pen moving. I have on occasion taken to repeatedly writing out, "I don't want to do this," or, "I don't know what to write." Do this a few times and new ideas will pop out.

If you try to stop and think about what to write next, you are defeating the point. Journaling allows what's deep inside of you to get out and onto the page. This is one of the best ways to peel away the layers.

Julia Cameron writes about this in her excellent book, "The Artist's Way." She calls it "morning pages," and, as you may have guessed from the name, she suggests doing this process in the morning before your mind has become cluttered with other things. Her method is to write out three full pages every morning. I have done this, and it is amazing what you can learn about yourself.

You can use any one of these methods, or all three. The important thing is to do something to get at the deeper you so that you can really start expressing yourself.

One of my best friends achieved a music degree in college, but then went on to get a good paying job in computers. He knew music would always be a part of his life, but it would just be something he did on the side – or maybe "someday" when the time would be right.

He started using these techniques (most specifically, journaling), and after two months he realized that he did not enjoy what he was doing and that he would be miserable if he didn't pursue music. He made the decision to go back to grad school and get a degree so that he could work as a composer. He graduated with a master's degree in film composition and is now working doing what he loves – writing music. He is much happier and satisfied with his life because he has found a way to express himself everyday in what he does for a living.

Why We Resist

If this is so important, why do so few people do it? The most obvious answer is that people are not aware of the importance. But now you know, so that's not an excuse!

Here are a few other reasons for resistance that may crop up:

- **Fear**

As mentioned above, you may be afraid to do this. It is possible that you may discover some things about yourself lying below the surface of which you were unaware. If you have been avoiding some things about your life, you may be afraid to have to face them. You may be fearful that by really discovering and expressing yourself you will have to acknowledge some mistake you have made, or that you will be forced into action. You may have grown comfortable in your current job. Maybe you'd rather not face the truth that you are doing something that will ultimately leave you unsatisfied. You don't want to feel the pressure of moving on, changing the status quo, and building a better and more satisfying life.

> *"If you are afraid of the process then you are exactly the person who must do it."*

While it sounds trite, if you are afraid of the process then you are exactly the person who **must** do it. Your fear indicates that there is something going on below the surface. In that case, you will never be fulfilled until you peel away the layers and uncover what it is.

- ## It's Hard

In many ways these processes, while simple, seem hard. Twenty minutes may feel like an eternity when you are meditating. Your life may be busy enough without adding 30 minutes of journaling every morning. If you have never done this sort of creative self-expression and flow, it may seem like a bit of a struggle in the beginning.

The key is to go back to the first principle in this book: Have fun! If you focus on the pain, time and difficulty, it will indeed seem like a struggle. If you try to do it "right," it will be a painful process. Just do your best, and be willing to make mistakes. That's how you learn, and doing something is better than doing nothing. The benefits of this journey far outweigh the initial difficulty of the process.

- ## Being Lonely

Amazingly enough, many people don't like to be alone with their thoughts. There are so many stimuli in the world that it may feel uncomfortably odd to be with no one (and therefore no stimulus) but yourself.

Wayne Dyer speaks about the difference between being lonely and being alone. I find there is a great distinction between them. When you are alone, no one else is with you. When you are lonely, you feel disconnected from everyone else. You can be alone and feel connected to others and the world. You can be in a crowded room and feel lonely.

A big factor in whether you feel lonely or just simply alone is how comfortable you are with your own thoughts. If you are not used to being alone, you may find it very uncomfortable to find yourself with only your own thoughts for company. It is like (or worse than) being with a person you don't know and with whom you don't communicate all that well. But, just like getting to know that other person, the more you get to know yourself the more comfortable you become, and the more you enjoy having that time to be alone with your thoughts.

Of all the sections in the book, this one may seem to have the least to do with improv comedy. However, for an experienced improviser, it is the most relevant. An improviser only brings himself to the stage. Only with a real understanding of himself and a real ability to express himself can he truly be great.

In the same way, until you truly understand yourself and are confidently willing to express yourself, you can never truly be great or satisfied in your own life.

Remember, to get free access to over 25 exercises and improv games to help practice these principles, visit
www.AvishParashar.com/bookbonus

Principle #4:

The Only Thing
We Have To Fear...

Fear is a major debilitating force in the world of improv comedy. Consider this bit from Jerry Seinfeld:

"According to most studies, people's number one fear is public speaking. Number two is death. Death is number two. Does that sound right? This means to the average person, if you go to a funeral, you're better off in the casket than doing the eulogy."

How do you think all those people who listed fear of public speaking as their number one fear would feel if you asked them to not only give a speech, but to do it *without a script??*

To stand in front of others with nothing prepared in advance is a scary proposition indeed. Unfortunately, the more a performer feels fear, the less likely he is to perform well. It becomes a self-fulfilling cycle.

Fear is deadly in improv comedy. It makes performers tentative, tight, and unwilling to do the things that are necessary to perform great improv. Things in your personal and professional lives are the same way. The more fear you feel, the less willing you will be to do the things that you need to do in order to succeed. When working with new improvisers, I spend a great deal of time getting them over fear. If you can overcome some of your key fears, you too will be able to "perform" better at whatever it is you want to do.

There are Many Types of Fear; Few are Valid

Fear can be a very useful thing. I am afraid to drive so fast that the car is a little out of control. Fear prevents me from running out into traffic or grabbing a hot pot handle. Fear of financial ruin keeps me working hard at my business. Fear is nature's way of keeping you safe and sound. Ignoring these fears makes you foolish. There are certain parts of the city I am afraid to walk around in late at night. That's a real fear, and to ignore it could get me into serious trouble. Unfortunately, we all have taken nature's lead and run with it to absurd extremes. These are the fake fears, and they fall into several categories:

Imagined Fears

Imagined fears are those fears of things that just don't exist. For example, as a child, were you ever afraid there was a monster in your closet? Even if your parents came in and checked it out, you may have still felt that fear. As a child, it's understandable to have these fears. Kids don't have the maturity and experience to distinguish between the real and imagined fears.

As adults, you would think that we have learned to distinguish between the real and imagined. But we haven't.

You may still have some imagined fears. They won't be as obvious as the monster in the closet, but they will still be there. For example, do you get incredibly self-conscious when you walk into a crowded room because you think everyone is looking at you? Are you resisting starting a business because you know for a fact that if you do the taxes will get so complicated that you certainly get into trouble with the IRS? Do you avoid asking questions in classes or meetings because you are afraid of looking stupid?

Ninety-nine percent of the time these are imagined fears. Most people aren't giving you a second glance when you walk in a room. Thousands of people have business that don't get into trouble with the IRS (hire a good accountant). And most times when you ask a question people will be respectful. Plus, there's a good chance that they need the answer to the same question.

Before you let a fear run your life, think it through to make sure it is a realistic one, not just an imagined one.

Anticipation Fears

Anticipation fears are the most common ones. If you have an event coming up that you are not sure about, you may find yourself stressing and getting afraid over what you think will happen.

These fears are incredibly destructive for two reasons:

1) They are Paralyzing.

You may find yourself unable to focus on other things that are important because your mind is so wrapped up in the fear.

For example, have you ever had your boss say to you, "we need to talk," and you set up an appointment for later in the day? If you are afraid that the boss is setting you up for bad news, you may find yourself having an extremely unproductive day as your mind flits about all the potential negative things that might happen. What if you get fired? What if you get transferred, or demoted?

The fact is that you don't know what's going to happen, so wasting time with fear isn't helping anyone. Also, by allowing the fear to paralyze you, you are stopping yourself from taking the actions necessary to prevent what you are afraid of from actually happening!

What do I mean by this? Imagine that you have a big presentation coming up, and you are afraid that the people in attendance will hate it. If you are paralyzed by fear, you will find it hard to focus on anything, much less working on the presentation. Of course working on the presentation to make it as good as possible is the only way to decrease the chances of the worst thing coming to pass. In this way, the more you give in to fear, the more reason you have to be afraid.

As I mentioned above, all fear is not bad. If you use the fear to motivate yourself to buckle down and focus and get to work, that's great. If you let it overwhelm you, that's not so good.

2) They Often Don't Come to Pass.

I once had a couple of members in my improv group ask to meet me to "talk about something." The meeting was set up for the next day. Over the next 24 hours I let such fear build up inside of me that I was essentially useless. I had it in my head that they were going to complain and lay me out (for what, I wasn't sure, but such is the way with fears – they don't always make sense).

When we actually got together, the conversation was very pleasant. It turns out they weren't meeting with me to yell at me. They were meeting with me to tell me that it was time for them to move on and leave the improv group. I wasted 24 hours of my life because I anticipated something that never came to pass. In fact, *they* were nervous because they thought I would be mad!

I'm sure this has happened to you. You are so sure that something bad is going to happen that you stress over the worst case scenario. Then, when the event comes to pass, it ends up not being nearly as bad as you thought it would be. Sometimes it may even end up being a positive thing.

Anticipation fears are the worst, because they are the reason that people do not try new things, or expand themselves, or grow and succeed.

Disproportionate Fears

Sometimes our fears are valid but are overblown. Most phobias fall into this category.

I'm not a psychologist or psychiatrist, so I'm not going to delve into phobias. However, think about it logically. Being afraid of snakes is a valid fear – poisonous snakes can kill you. However, being too afraid to look at a snake behind a sealed pane of glass at a zoo, or to see one on TV, is disproportionate.

If you have a legitimate phobia, I am not decrying you – you should seek professional help. However, sometimes we make fears much bigger in our minds than they should be.

For example, many people have a fear of cold calling. Having a fear is different than not liking it. If you don't like cold calling you find ways of not doing it, but if you must, you do it. Having a fear of it means that your heart beats faster even thinking about it, you start to sweat as you dial the phone, and your voice conveys fear when you talk to a prospect (if you get that far).

This is a disproportionate fear. The worst thing that will happen on a cold call is that someone will hang up on you. Actually, they could laugh at you and tell you that you will never succeed in your business and you should give up, which is what happened to me on one call, but that's another story. Even in that awful example, how bad is that really? It doesn't affect you or your business.

Weighed against the potential upside – money, income, success – that fear seems miniscule. And yet that is a fear that holds many people back.

A simple way to see if your fear is disproportionate is to ask, "What's the worst that could happen?" Don't cop out on me here either – what's the worst that could realistically happen? Then ask yourself how bad that worst case situation really is. Compare those answers to the scenario of whatever your fear is preventing from happening. Once you answer those questions, it will be pretty clear whether your fear is proportionate or not.

Why This is Important

Fear is the single biggest limiting factor people face in succeeding and achieving what they say they want. Fear has the following affects:

1) Fear Stops You Before You Start.

This is the most common and deadly outcome of fear. Whether it's fear of failure, rejection, the unknown, or anything else, being afraid is what keeps people locked in their comfort zones.

Think back to anything in your life that you wanted to do (or want to do) but have not done yet. Chances are that there is fear in there somewhere.

2) Fear Reduces Your Effectiveness.

As described in the "anticipation fears" section above, when you focus on your fear you reduce the energy and concentration you put into the task at hand. As such, you end up doing worse job than you might otherwise have done, thus realizing your fears.

3) Fear is Physically Dangerous.

While this may be outside the scope of this book, fear can actually hurt you. Stress, high-blood pressure, anxiety attacks, etc., are physical manifestations of fear which serve to break down your health.

4) Fear is Demoralizing.

The more you let your actions be guided by fear, the worse you feel about yourself. This results in less energy and motivation to do or try anything. It is an unfortunate downward spiral.

Taking action in the face of fear, no matter how small, is incredibly motivating. Once you start this path, your self-esteem increases and you develop momentum. But it has to start with one small step.

How to Overcome the Fear

Fear is obviously a dangerous and limiting thing. So how do you move from a place of being afraid to a place of taking action?

Here are a few ideas:

Act as if Until You are

"Fake it until you make it!" This is great piece of advice. Even if you are afraid, if you act as if you aren't, you will actually find yourself feeling less afraid. In practical sense, what that means is not allowing yourself to give in to fear. When people are afraid, they do some specific things that demonstrate and increase that fear.

For example, scared people talk about their fears, and tell themselves and others how afraid they are. To "fake it," just make sure that you don't do that. You don't have to brag about how non-afraid you are (that would be bravado), just don't indulge your fear.

Fear has an affect on how you carry your body – scared people get fidgety, slump their shoulders, and have trouble making eye contact. To act confident, reverse these traits: control your movements and slow down, stand up straight, and make good eye contact.

It seems too simple, but it's true: by donning the outward trappings of confidence you can make yourself feel less afraid. Eventually, you may even forget what you were scared about in the first place!

To be clear, when I say "fake it" I mean fake confidence. I do not mean to fake or lie about who you are. For example, if you are afraid because you are walking into a meeting with 8 PhDs and you never finished high school, faking it doesn't mean that you claim to have a Harvard degree. It just means that you walk into that room pretending that you are the most confident person in the world.

Dale Carnegie's Approach to Worry and Fear

Dale Carnegie was an extremely famous expert on communication and personal development. His book, 'How to Win Friends and Influence People' is considered one of the ultimate books on success and interaction. The Dale Carnegie & Associates organization offers personal development courses all across the world.

"By donning the outward trappings of confidence you can make yourself feel less afraid."

Carnegie had another book, 'How to Stop Worrying and Start Living.' He wrote some very nice strategies to get over worry and to put fear into perspective. I'd like to share one that he mentions in the early part of his book. This technique contains three steps.

First, ask yourself, 'What's the worst that could happen.' Be honest and blunt. Don't exaggerate, but don't sugar coat.

Second, prepare to accept the worst if you have to. Once you have decided to accept the worst if it happens, your worry immediately diminishes. This is due in part to the fact that once you have decided to accept the worst, you stop wasting time and energy hoping it doesn't happen.

Third, once you accept the worst, calmly begin improving upon it. Start devising strategies to make sure the worst doesn't happen. Once you have done step two, you can really start to come up with new and better solutions.

Let's take a hypothetical example. Suppose you have a huge project due, and you don't think you'll be able to finish it in the time allotted. At first, you spend a lot of time stressing over the impossibility of the task. You think about the project day and night, and it is driving you crazy.

Now, apply the Carnegie method to it. First, what's the worst that could happen? Well, you could get fired and be out of job. Maybe you have a family and a mortgage, so being fired would be very bad.

Second, prepare to accept it. If you did get fired, what would you do? You could collect unemployment and throw yourself 100% into finding a new job. You could cut back on expenses and luxuries for a while. You could get some short term temp work to pay some bills. You could sell some of your possessions. You could move and sell the house. None of these are enticing scenarios, but you should realize that you could handle the worst case in some way, if it happens. The interesting thing is that once you accept it, you immediately feel better.

Third, start improving on the worst case. How could you prevent getting fired? You could talk to your boss about the deadline. You could make sure that the key parts of the project get done and ignore the less important parts. Or, you could do a so-so job across the board, just to get it done (not the best answer, but hey, I'm trying to save your house!). You could get help on the project. You could work evenings and weekends.

Once you've gone through the process, you feel better and you start using you energy on solutions. Try it sometime, and see if it helps you.

Take Little Steps

One of the key reasons fears overwhelm us is that we lose perspective. We make the tasks to overcome the fear so big in our heads that we get paralyzed. We also tend to overlook the small steps and victories that might lead to long term change.

For example, if you have a fear of public speaking, when you envision taking an action to overcome it don't picture yourself in front of a large crowd speaking for 45 minutes. If that's your picture, it's no surprise that you're afraid!

We are instant gratification creatures; we want to eat the whole enchilada in one bite. Unfortunately, that never works. Instead, we are far better served by breaking the task down into small steps that still push us, but don't overwhelm us.

In the speaking example, if you have a major issue with it, perhaps you should start with something tiny like speaking up to ask a question in class. Or maybe your first little step could be to do a 30-second introduction for another speaker at a small meeting (such as a service club or any group that involves you). Taking that one little step will not destroy your fear instantaneously, which is why people scoff at them. Don't do that! Pat yourself on the back and reward yourself for taking even the smallest of steps. You don't need to overcome it all at once – you just need to overcome it eventually.

Think in Terms of Abundance vs. Scarcity

A key limiting idea that feeds our fears is thinking in terms of scarcity. If you believe that the things you value in life (love, relationships, happiness, money, comfort, etc) are scarce, then you will be very afraid to take any chances because you will be afraid to lose what you do have.

If, on the other hand, you come from a place of abundance, you will be much freer in your actions. Coming from a place of abundance simply means that you believe that there is always more out there – you can find more love, more happiness, new relationships, more money, etc.

Fear of loss is a huge reason people don't try new things. What's odd though is that if something is so easy to lose, did you ever really have it to begin with? The irony here is that the more you believe in abundance and aren't afraid of loss, the less likely you are to lose the things you already have.

Principle #5:

Get Out There and Fail

Yes, you read that correctly. You need to get out there and fail!

For most people, failure is considered a negative thing; something to be avoided at all costs. Unfortunately, by avoiding failure, people end up limiting their success. Now, before you get overly excited about how easy this task is, you need to know one important thing – you can't go out and try to fail. You have to be trying to succeed.

I touched upon this point in the earlier chapter on "Willingness." You have to try to succeed but be willing to fail. Now let's explore more than that. In order to succeed, you must fail!

Why This is Important

This is a vital principle that not only gets missed, but unfortunately, is actively put down.

Consider this: from the moment we get into school, we are taught that failure is a bad thing. Everything gets graded, and the worst grade is an "F," which stands for "Fail."

Our parents, out of love and with the hope they were doing what was best for us, reinforced the idea of how bad failure is. Teachers, administrators, well meaning family and friends, all did their best to motivate, guide, intimidate, and teach us to not fail.

On one level this is a good lesson. I am not saying doing well is a bad thing – quite the contrary. Doing well is great! I want and expect everyone with whom I work to be striving to succeed at the highest level.

The problem is, the overemphasis on failure creates a mentality that failure is a bad thing and something to avoid. The irony is that the more you fail the more likely you are to succeed.

On an improv stage, performers have a huge desire to "play it safe." They don't try new ideas, and sometimes even fall back on old jokes that have worked before (I hate it when they do that!). I always tell performers, "I'd rather have you try something and fail then play it safe and succeed." I had this approach not just in rehearsals and classes, but in live performances as well. Many people are comfortable taking some chances in a very safe environment, but put them into a real scenario and they fall back on old patterns. While the classroom is a great place to learn and practice, the only real growth happens in the real world.

> "The irony is that the more you fail the more likely you are to succeed."

You might be thinking, "Why do you want your performers to fail?" I don't – I want them to succeed. I actually hate it when something fails in a live show because it sets things back and we have to recover from a game that clearly bombed.

However, I understand the process. If someone does something on stage and fails it's a giant pain, but it's a necessary pain. The short term difficulty of failing on stage is far outweighed by the long term gains of cultivating that mindset. (I'll spare you from the clichéd "working out and having sore muscles now for health and fitness later" analogy…)

What are the gains? Here are a few:

Failure is Often the Lead-In to Success

The only way to be sure never to fail is to never try anything. Many people approach life determining they will not try new things until they are sure they will succeed. Regrettably, that time never comes. However, failure can lead to success *if handled properly*. Many people tend to handle failure poorly. When they fail, they may get angry or depressed or just give up.

The better way to handle failure is to find some success in it and look at it as a learning opportunity. Rather than getting down on yourself for failing, be happy with yourself for trying. Instead of getting angry, get curious: "What can I learn from this? Why did I fail this time? What can I do to make sure I don't fail next time?"

Once you have asked and answered these questions, take action on the answers! Failure is, in fact, bad if you don't learn from it, and if you don't change your actions or try something new as a result of the failure. Then you are doomed to fail again.

With the right attitude and an intelligent approach, failure can be the key to your success.

Indicator of Success

Failure can also be an indicator of impending success. What does that mean? Well, if you are failing in the right way, then that just may mean that success is right around the corner. If you are handling failure intelligently, as mentioned above, then the more you fail and adjust, the faster you will reach the goal you want. Remember, the only way to avoid failing is to never try anything. If you are failing, at least you are trying.

As with fear, many people get paralyzed by failure. They try once and fail, then try again a few weeks later. They fail again, then try a few months later. In the span of six months they may try and fail only two or three times. They then give up concluding, "I'll never succeed."

That is far too long between failures! If you want to succeed faster, go out there, try to succeed, but be willing to fail. Fail two or three times a day, learn from each experience, and in a very short period of time you will be far more successful!

Pushing Through & Quitting

In spiritual terms, failure is the universe's way of testing us. While it shouldn't be true, it is: the more difficult a thing is to come by, the more we appreciate it.

> *"Treat each failure as a test. Are you willing to get up, learn, and push harder?"*

Treat each failure as a test. Are you willing to get up, learn, and push harder? If not, then one of two things is true: 1) You don't really want what you were after all that much; or, 2) You don't deserve it.

That may sound harsh, but it's true. The universe is testing you to see if you deserve what you want. Push through the failure and you will prove to yourself and the universe that you deserve it. Chances are you will savor your success that much more.

Growth

More growth comes from failure than from success. Why is that? When you succeed, you usually don't take the time to analyze and examine what you're doing – you take it for granted.

When you fail, that's when you learn and analyze. To overcome failure, you also must change something – your approach, actions, or beliefs. This change is growth, and this change rarely happens when you succeed at everything.

I am not getting down on succeeding. I just feel that if you are doing nothing but succeeding then chances are that you are holding yourself back and not trying enough. If you are not failing at anything and are perfectly happy with everything in your life, then that's great for you. If it is true though, I doubt you would be reading this book...

Be Sensible

Let's take a step back and silence the little (or big) voice in your head screaming, "But failing has consequences!"

Yes, failing does have consequences. When I say, "Get out there and fail," I don't mean for you to be stupid. Don't go off half-cocked with a crazy business idea lose all your money and be unable to pay your bills. Don't walk into your boss's office and demand a raise if you haven't taken the steps to determine whether you actually feel you deserve it. Don't start an affair with your married friend just to prove that you are willing to fail.

There's smart failure and stupid failure. Smart failure is when you think things through and take action in line with your goals, and with the knowledge that if you fail, you will be ok. (If you forgot how to do this, re-read the last chapter on fear).

Stupid failure is when you don't think things through, act in a way that may seem good in the moment, and then can't deal with the consequences of failure.

There are legitimate reasons to not fail. Most things that are holding you back however, come from the desperate desire to avoid failing. That desire was instilled in you as a child, and if you want to really succeed, it's time to let that desire go.

Detach From the Outcome

The primary reason people avoid failure is because of *excessive attachment to the outcome*. That is, we all get way too caught up in wanting things to work out well. One of the difficult ironies of life is that the more you want something to happen, the less likely it is to happen.

If you've ever played (or even watched) sports, you can relate to this phenomenon. When you are just playing for fun and don't care that much about winning and losing, you end up playing very well. In important games, it's easy to "tighten up" and play much worse. This is why it is so difficult to be a top athlete: many people can play extremely well; very few can play that well when millions of people are watching and the championship is on the line.

Does this mean that you shouldn't want anything? Well, if you're a Buddhist then you know that the key to happiness is to let go of desire...but don't worry, I'm not going to take it that far! It is fine to know what you want, and it is fine to want to succeed, achieve, or get something. To overcome that fear of failure and get out and do it you must just let go of the outcome.

The thought process of a person who thinks like this is, "I want to succeed, and I'm going to do my best, but if I fail, I fail. I know I can get up and try again." One way to detach from the outcome is to keep your focus on the here and now. Rather than thinking obsessively about your goal (which creates a huge attachment) focus on the steps you are taking now to achieve that goal.

This does fly in the face of what many self-improvement gurus may say. The common advice is to think all the time about your goals, and to post them everywhere around your house. I am all for visualizations and focusing on your goals to keep you on the right path. However, the fastest way to traverse that path is to fail, and fail a lot, and that will be impossible if you are too attached to the outcome.

Redefining the Rules of Success and Failure

Another reason people avoid failure is that they have set themselves up to never feel good. As an improv comedy teacher, I am constantly trying to reinforce the idea that having a bad scene or improv game is not failure. Not taking chances and playing it safe is failure. In this way, I have changed the rules of success and failure.

Most of us have rules for what it means to fail. In areas of our lives where we are not excelling, our rules are too stringent. "If I don't succeed perfectly the first time I try I have failed," is a common one. You may not say it that literally, but that is usually underlying our fear.

That rule is ludicrous, yet it is extremely common. No one is going to embark on something new and do it perfect the first time. You probably won't do it perfectly the one hundredth time (if ever)! A much better rule is, "if I try my best, regardless of what happens, I succeeded."

Similarly, many people have the rule, "I must do everything right to be a success." Again, and especially for big undertakings, the possibility of doing everything right is very small. A much better rule is, "As long as I learn from what I am doing wrong, I am succeeding."

Take a look at the areas in your own life where you are not succeeding or where you feel like a failure. Examine your own rules around failure and success and see if you can come up with new ones to accelerate your progress.

Fail Spectacularly

Since we know that if we try often, we will, on occasion, fail, I say, if you're going to fail, fail huge!!

I was reading an article about screenplay writing (from wordplayer.com) that was informing about this idea, and it referred to the movie "Raiders of the Lost Ark." Harrison Ford's character in that movie, Indiana Jones, can be considered the quintessential action hero.

And yet, if you analyze the events in the movie, you realize one thing: Indiana Jones fails at almost everything he does! Think about it. He loses the idol in the opening, burns down the bar, loses Marion, loses the Ark (twice!), and doesn't get to see what's in it. Then, in the end, the government takes the Ark away. Indiana Jones is one giant failure.

However, we never think about him as a failure because he does it so spectacularly. Jones tries so hard and works so hard every step of the way that we don't even notice that he's failing. And, even though he doesn't get to keep the Ark for his museum, in the end he still gets what he wants: the Nazis don't have the Ark to use as a weapon.

"Raiders of the Lost Ark" is just a movie, but I think the lessons of spectacular failure are useful. I want to make one thing clear – failing spectacularly doesn't mean ruining your life. In order to really adopt this principle you need to put real failure in perspective.

In improv terms, I always encourage performers to take big risks and if they fail, to fail big. I always prefer that a performer push herself and mess up rather than play it safe and appear to succeed.

In improv, this works because the worst that happens if you mess up is you end the scene and move on and maybe the audience doesn't like you. Of course, if you fail spectacularly the audience will like you.

In life and business, there are times to play it safe. Don't bet the retirement fund at the roulette table. Don't invest all of your company's profits in a risky new launch. However, there are many, many areas of life where we don't take action, or we take very conservative action because we are afraid of failing. We don't open our mouths for fear of losing a prospect. We don't try out for a play or hop up and do karaoke because we are afraid of looking silly. We don't walk across the room and say 'hi' to that certain someone because we are afraid of rejection.

If you are willing to fail spectacularly, two things will happen:

1) You Will Actually Succeed More Often

Just like in the section on willingness to fail, the more you throw yourself into the task the less likely you are to fail at it.

2) You Will Tap Into the Zest of Life

Think about some of your favorite stories about you and your friends. I'm sure many, if not most of them, revolve around some spectacular failures. If you can get to a place where you are willing to fail like this and laugh about it, your life will quickly fill with rich stories and experiences – of both failures and success.

The one other thing to keep in mind from Indiana Jones is that while he failed throughout, he kept pushing forward. In the end, he got what he wanted. If you stay willing to fail spectacularly and keep pushing ahead, you too will ultimately get what you want.

The Resolute Acceptance of Death

Miyamoto Musashi was a 16th century Samurai and is considered to be the greatest swordsman who ever lived. After fighting in over sixty duels, Musashi reflected on the concept of strategy and what allowed him to win so many battles. He recorded these thoughts in a book titled 'Go Rin No Sho' – or, in English, 'A Book of Five Rings.'

So why am I talking about sword fighting now? Well, because the book itself uses sword fighting as a metaphor for all things. The book is about strategy in general. It is considered such a masterpiece of strategy that some business schools, including Harvard, use it to teach business strategy.

In terms of improvisation and what lessons we can take from it now, I would like to quote one line from the book. Musashi says, "The way of the warrior is the resolute acceptance of death." These eleven words are profound and contain the secret to a great many successes. The statement means that in order to do his best, a warrior must accept the possibility and reality of death. A warrior who did not do this would be afraid of

"Once you accept the reality of failure, you free up your energy to allow yourself to perform to the best of your ability."

dying in combat, and as such would lessen his ability to fight. Ironically, the more concerned a warrior was with dying, the more likely he was to die. Only by accepting the reality of death could a warrior get past it.

Taken outside of feudal Japan, this sentiment can have a huge impact on your success in a variety of areas. Like the warrior, rather than fearing the negative consequence, once you embrace and accept it as a real possibility you can move past it.

In a performing sense, if you are afraid of doing poorly, the audience will sense it and you will do poorly. If, however, you say to yourself, "I don't care. I might mess it up, but if I do, I do. I'll just go out and focus on doing the best I can," you'll find yourself performing immensely well.

The same rule applies to anything in life. The more you are afraid of messing up a presentation, or a project, or taking up a new hobby, or talking to somebody new, the more likely you are to mess it up. Once you accept the reality of failure, you free up your energy to allow yourself to perform to the best of your ability.

Remember, all you have to accept is failure, or rejection, or embarrassment – Musashi had to accept death.

Remember, to get free access to over 25 exercises and improv games to help practice these principles, visit
www.AvishParashar.com/bookbonus

Principle #6:

Stay In the Moment

Staying in the moment is one the most powerful things an improviser can do. It is also one of the most amazing things you can do to be more connected and more effective in any task or endeavor.

In improv comedy, a performer is constantly creating things on the spot. To an outside observer, it may appear that brilliant improvisers start a scene with a clear idea of where everything is going to go, and then they get there. Nothing could be farther from the truth! Great improvisers start their scenes, and they may have an idea of where things are going, but they are absolutely willing to abandon their ideas and flow. If they are doing their jobs right, they will pretty much have to do this.

The only way they can do this effectively is if they stay in the moment. That is, it is fine to have an idea of where things are headed, but the only thing you really have is the present, so you have to make the most of it.

What exactly does staying in the moment mean? It means that you don't dwell on the past, or stress over the future. It means that when you are doing a task, you put all of your attention on the task at hand. If you are writing, you shut off all distractions and write. You also clear your head of other ideas, priorities, etc. If you are speaking with someone, you stop thinking about what happened earlier, or what you have to get done later. If you are exercising, you focus on the workout and not on how you have to finish soon to get back to work.

While this sounds simple and obvious, it is extremely hard for most people. In this world, we are all always looking for the next thing we have to do, or thinking way too much about a past event.

Oddly enough, we tend to think that by stressing about the past or future that we are somehow "dealing" with it. It is as if by giving it our attention, we are working on it. This is why some people stress over everything, and make tension where there doesn't need to be any (you know who you are!). Many people have the fear that if we put our problems out of our heads temporarily, that we are somehow being negligent.

The reverse is actually true. By staying in the moment and putting your attention on whatever it is you are doing, you are making yourself more efficient and effective. When you focus 100%, you will get more done then if you split your focus. This means that you will get your tasks done in less time, and therefore have more time later to focus on other things.

"By staying in the moment and putting your attention on whatever it is you are doing, you are making yourself more efficient and effective."

Have you ever been overwhelmed; where you have multiple high-stress things to handle? The challenge in these cases is that when you tackle one high-stress item your mind reminds you how, by taking care of this one thing, you are neglecting all the other important things in your life. In this instance, the desire to "shut down" can be strong. This is a natural reaction, but it is also the worst one!

You must remind yourself that you can only effectively do one thing at a time. Pick the one that is the most important, and commit to focusing on it 100%, even though it means other things will not get done. The way to get out of that feeling of being overwhelmed isn't to do everything at once, but rather to get things done systematically, one at a time.

In relationships, this can be looked at as the difference between quality and quantity. Some people spend the entire evening, every evening, with their families, and yet they still feel disconnected. Others are very busy and can only squeak out an hour or so, and yet they end up being very connected. This is because what you do and how involved you are, is as important as how much total time you spend. Five hours in the same room as someone, sitting and watching TV, is going to be less effective than 30 minutes of a real conversation.

The first step in increasing your productivity, efficiency, connection, and happiness is to practice staying in the moment.

By staying in the moment, you get some nice benefits:

Rapport and Connection

Staying in the present allows you to listen and give 100% of yourself to whomever you are speaking. You have probably been in a conversation with someone who was clearly preoccupied. How did it feel? It probably didn't feel all that great. If you stop focusing on the future or past, you create rapport and connection with the present.

Impulses

An interesting thing happens when you stay in the moment. You actually start to pay attention to your gut instincts, or, as I call them, "impulses." It's ironic, but the more you get out of your own head, the more you recognize the impulses your subconscious is giving you.

These impulses can come in the form of ideas, observations, insights, or questions. The next time you are speaking with someone, stay in the moment and don't think ahead. As the conversation goes on, you will start to come up with things to say and questions to ask based entirely on what your partner is saying. Don't dwell on these ideas (or you will be right back in your head) but simply use them to keep the conversation going and to get more information.

This will take practice. If you are used to really thinking a lot about things, you will find it very hard to keep your mind quiet. Then, when you get an impulse, your first instinct will be to judge, evaluate, or act immediately upon it. Practice resisting the urge to do any of these things. Rather, acknowledge the thought and then go back to listening. At some point, it will be your turn to speak and that is when you can use the thoughts your mind has given you.

In improv, this kind of empty-minded focus combined with listening to impulses is what leads to brilliant performance. It takes time, and an improviser has to trust himself, but when he does some wonderful stuff happens.

In the same way, you will need to let go and trust yourself. You must be willing to practice. When you do, some wonderful things will happen for you.

Communicate More Effectively

Staying in the moment is the ultimate key to effective communication. There are classes on speaking, conveying your message, body language, active listening, personality typing, and more. I find that all that becomes relatively meaningless (or just a nice bonus) if you are willing to stay in the moment.

Staying in the moment applies to both sides of the communication coin: listening and speaking.

The only thing that blocks effective listening is that people allow other thoughts into their minds. When someone is speaking to you, if you are paying attention to the thoughts in your head, you are not listening. These thoughts could be respectful (you may be thinking over what they just said while they are continuing to speak), disrespectful (your mind may wander to other things in your life), or argumentative (you may be thinking of your response instead of listening to what your partner is saying).

Regardless of the underlying cause, if you are wrapped up in your thoughts, you can not listen 100% effectively. If you pay attention to your partner instead of your thoughts, you will automatically become a "great listener" and an effective communicator.

Staying out of your head and in the moment when you are speaking is much harder than when you are listening, but it is the key to properly conveying your message.

Have you ever been in a conversation with someone who goes on and on to you about something that you are not particularly interested in? They probably have a great passion for what they are saying but they have not picked up on the fact that you are not interested. While they are talking, you're thinking, "My God, won't you shut up! I'm not interested!" This is because when most people speak they go into their own heads and get wrapped up in what they are saying. By getting wrapped up in their words, they stop paying attention to the listener, and as a result end up annoying or boring people.

If you can pay attention to the other person while you are speaking, you will be able to see whether he is interested or not. You will also see whether or not he understands. Sometimes people may not follow you but they won't say anything out of embarrassment.

Paying attention while you speak also allows you to adjust as you go to make sure the person is interested and understands. This is a vital tool, especially if you do any persuasive speaking (sales, project pitching, opinion speaking, etc).

To be a more effective communicator, you can read tons of books, take hours of classes and learn dozens of techniques, or you can just practice emptying your thoughts and staying in the moment. The choice is yours.

Be Open to Opportunities

When you stay in the moment, you open yourself to all the opportunities that would otherwise pass you by. Do you know someone who is "lucky?" He seems to be in the right place at the right time, and opportunities just seem to find him? Chances are that person is good at staying in the moment, at least in that area

"The first step to opening up many new doors is to start noticing them."

of his life. Opportunities are all around you. But if you are walking around wrapped up in thoughts of the past or future, you will miss all of them.

How many people do you walk by that would be beneficial for you to meet, personally or professionally? How many businesses, flyers, stores, events, etc., do you walk past not even realizing that they are there? Have you ever gone down the same street over and over and then one day a friend takes you to a place on that street and you say, "Hmmm, I never even knew this was here?"

Opportunities are everywhere. The first step to opening up many new doors is to start noticing them (the second step is to take action on them, but that's in a later chapter). The only way to do that is to get out of your head, stay in the moment, and pay attention to the world around you.

Understand the Difference Between Attention and Intention

When it comes to staying in the moment, the key is to understand the difference between where your attention is and where your intention is.

From the dictionary:

Attention: Concentration of the mental powers upon an object; a close or careful observing or listening.

Intention: Course of action that one plans on following.

From these definitions, it is obvious that attention takes place in the present, and intention concerns itself with the future. And yet, most people reverse them and get into trouble. In improv, performers are trained to put all of their concentration on the present; to stay in the moment and work with the people around them. At the same time, they need to be clear on their intentions. They must have an idea of where the scene and action will go. As we have previously seen, an improviser must be willing to let go of that intention when things change (and that point create a new intention).

Time after time, unfortunately, performers reverse the roles. They put their attention on the future and their intentions in the present. An improviser may start a scene and focus heavily on where the scene will ultimately lead. By doing this, she is putting her attention on the future, and not on the people around her. By focusing single-mindedly on where she wants to go, she then tries to force things in that direction. Therefore, her intention is in the present. She intends for people to flow with her right now.

This unfortunate reversal happens often in life. A person in an unpleasant situation will put his intention on the now and his attention on the future. For example, take two people who hate their jobs. Let's call them Steve and John.

Steve is unhappy, and he spends his time lamenting about how awful things are and how he wished it was different. If one of his co-workers does something to upset him (which happens quite often) he gets angry and complains about how she should do things differently. He spends a great deal of his time wishing and daydreaming of a better job.

John is also unhappy. He also dreams of a better job, but he doesn't spend all day daydreaming. Instead, he focuses on researching other job opportunities, and he enrolls in a night class to improve his "marketability." John's co-workers also often upset him, but instead of wishing they were different, he uses it as fuel to be more productive in his job search.

So what's the difference between these two?

Steve is clearly putting his attention on the future. Daydreaming and wishing don't accomplish anything. At the same time, his complaining is indicative of the fact that he is trying to change things he cannot. His intention is in the present.

John has a much healthier approach. While his intention is in the future ("I will get a new job soon.") his attention is on the present ("What can I do now to get a new job?").Who do you think is going to get a new job first?

It doesn't take a rocket scientist to see that in this example Steve is more negative and John is more positive. This balance between intention and attention is one of the key things that sets positive people apart from negative people.

Think of a situation in your life that makes you unhappy. If it's persistent, it is likely that you have your intention and attention reversed. Try switching it up, and see how that helps.

Get Out of Your Own Head and Pay Attention to The World and People Around You

The primary obstacle people face when it comes to staying in the moment is that they are walking around wrapped up in their own heads. We all have thoughts inside of us constantly. When we walk down the street, our minds are racing with all the things that have happened in the past or that are going to happen in the future. When we work on a project we often are thinking of other projects or other things going on in our lives. Sometimes when we are talking with someone, our thoughts will be in our own heads instead of on the conversation!

If you are wrapped up in your own head and thoughts then you are definitely not staying in the moment. There is so much going on in the world around you at any given moment, that to not pay attention to it is to short change both yourself and the people you are with.

For some reason we feel that if we dwell on something that we are "dealing with it." Many people even feel guilty if they get their mind off of the major issues in their lives to focus on other things.

I am not saying that you should ignore the major issues in your life. However, if you want to maximize your productivity and effectiveness, you have o realize that "dwelling" is not a solution. Dwelling is just a way that fools us into thinking we are doing something, when in fact all it is doing is reducing our ability to be effective in other areas.

Next time you are interacting with someone and find your thoughts wander, commit to refocusing and putting your attention back on them. When you are working on a project and find yourself thinking on other things or "multi-tasking," commit to pushing those thoughts aside and focusing 100% on what you are working on. The next time you are walking on the street take a few minutes to stop thinking so much and just pay attention to the world around you – it will be quite an experience.

Keep a Zen Mind

Improv, to me, is a very Zen sort of thing.

Zen is an eastern mindset that focuses on emptying the mind, reflecting, and being in the moment as opposed to thinking or struggling for answers.

When most people see improv comedians perform, at least good ones, they are dazzled by the wit and cleverness that they see. This style of observation is one of the most destructive obstacles to getting more people involved in improvisation.

Improv is not about being clever, witty, or funny. It is really about being in the moment, being honest, and being yourself.

I was once teaching an improv class and I was taking the students through a simple creativity exercise where the goal was to say the first thing that came into their heads, regardless of how "good" the idea was. One student said, "I have trouble because I am trying to think of the "right" thing – I mean, we need to come up with a good idea right?"

The answer is no. Great improvisers don't necessarily come up with great or good ideas. They stay in the moment and come up with a simple idea, and then, by using their talents and skills, they build off of the basic idea until something wonderful and great forms. The faster you embrace this idea into your own life, the easier life will become. How many times do you wait to do something because you can't figure it all out? Or, are you waiting around for a great idea to form?

Like most people I have many friends with varying degrees of closeness. With my closest friends, I don't need to have any plans at all. We just get together, and even if we do nothing but hang out at one of our houses, we have an amazing time. With other friends, I feel like we always need "plans." We can't just get together. We need to know what we are going to do. These are people I like very much, but I don't think I will ever be exceptionally close to them.

While it's great to experience all that life has to offer, and to travel and do many different things, the person who will be truly fulfilled will be the one who can find joy in simplicity.

Now that's a Zen thought...

Empty Your Mind of Thoughts

This is not a book on Zen. For our purposes, all we are going to get into is the concept of having an open and empty mind.

I love improv because at this point, it is so much easier than scripted work. When done right, you don't have to think when improvising. You just stay open and empty and something wonderful happens. This is a wonderful place to be, but it is a hard place to get to as a new improviser. Because of fear and conditioning, most people have a very hard time letting go and not desperately trying to "think" while on stage.

The key is to empty your mind. What that means is to simply clear your head of thoughts, and just be in the moment. This is incredibly hard to do, especially if you have never tried it before.

This empty mind concept will reappear in many sections of this book, from creativity to communication to goal setting and more. For now, just take a few moments to try to empty your head of all thoughts and see how hard it is for you.

Sneaking Up On a Mirror

When I was heavily involved in the martial arts, I used to attend seminars pretty regularly. At these seminars, one or more very high ranking, experienced masters would teach techniques and skills. It was a great way to learn directly from people who had pioneered some of these art forms. In addition to that, there were always high ranking instructors walking around to help and share. At one such seminar, an instructor came up to help me and my partner. He was an amazing martial artist, and had some wonderful ideas. But I have to admit, he said some things that I just didn't understand until (literally) years later.

One such comment was "You can't sneak up on a mirror." He even went to the length of acting out sneaking up on a mirror and failing, and he also encouraged us to try (I didn't; I just took his word on it). At the time, I felt like he was saying something profound, but I didn't know what on earth he meant by it.

A year or two later, I was teaching an improv rehearsal, and I was talking about how important it is to be fast and to not over-think things; how creativity comes from the subconscious and not the conscious. In a flash, it hit me: that's what was meant by "not being able to sneak up on a mirror!"

A mirror is empty and purely reflective. As such, it reacts in an instant. As soon as you look in the mirror, you see yourself. On the flip side, you have probably had the experience of being "lost in thought" and someone walks right up to you and you don't realize it until they say something.

The lesson here is that thought limits reflex. The more you are thinking, the less able you are to respond quickly and with creativity. For a martial artist, this means that the more you are thinking about what your attack will be, the less able you will be to deal with your opponent's attacks. For an improviser, this means that the more you think about what you want to do or where you want the scene to go, the less able you are to work with your partners and create something spontaneous and amazing.

For an individual trying to succeed in life, this means that the more wrapped up in your own thoughts you are the less likely you are to notice and take advantage of all the wonderful opportunities around you.

Empty Your Cup

There is a Zen story that I really like:

Once upon a time there was a very learned professor who wanted to learn about Zen, so he sought out a famous Zen master. The Zen master was more than happy to talk with the professor. When the two got together, the Zen master tried to explain the various ideas about Zen. Every time he would start in on an idea though, the professor would immediately jump in with his own thoughts, as if he was trying to show how much he knew.

Finally, the Zen Master suggested that they take a break, and he made some tea. He first poured tea into the professor's cup. He filled the cup all the way to the top, but then he kept pouring. The cup overflowed, but the Master kept pouring. Eventually, the professor could not contain himself and yelled, "Enough! The cup is full and can't take anymore!"

The Zen Master stopped pouring and smiled at the professor. "Like this cup, your mind is so full that there is no room for new ideas. In order for you to learn from me, you must first empty your cup."

This is one of the best lessons you can ever learn when it comes to new experiences and learning. You have accumulated a wealth of knowledge and experience, and you should never forget that. However, when you are in a new situation or trying to learn from someone else, be willing to "empty your cup" and open your mind to really get the most out of the experience.

Wrapping Up the Zen

Yes, there was a great deal of "Zen" in this chapter. But that's because the Zen concepts at their core are very much about letting go of thoughts and staying in the moment. Try some of them out yourself, and see how they work for you.

Remember, to get free access to over 25 exercises and improv games to help practice these principles, visit **www.AvishParashar.com/bookbonus**

Principle #7:

Tap Your Creativity

To be an improv comedian you must be able to tap your creativity. You take the stage with nothing prepared and then create comedy and theater on the spot.

I chose the words above carefully. I did not say, "To be an improv comedian you must *be creative.*" I said, "You must be able to tap your creativity." The distinction is critical.

Most people think that improvisers are naturally creative. The corollary to that belief is that they assume that they are not creative. Nothing could be further from the truth. All people have the potential for great creativity. People whom we see as naturally creative just learned how to tap into it somewhere along the way. They probably don't even know what they are doing since they have been "creative" all their lives. In the same way, people who don't consider themselves creative assume they can't be because they never learned how and are now stuck in their ways.

The truth is that creativity is natural, and everyone has it. Take a look at young children at play. They are immensely creative, and they don't lose that creativity until society (parents, teachers, friends or fellow students, etc) makes them self-conscious with recriminations ("Don't do that."; "Don't say that."; "Grow up!").

To recapture your creativity, think about it as a skill that can be learned rather than an innate ability. Once you understand and practice the process, you will be able to unleash your own creativity.

Why This is Important

When I start talking about creativity, some people shut their minds off. They assume that creativity is only concerned with writing, or painting, or music. While those things all require creativity, they fall into a subset of creativity called artistry. Don't confuse creativity with artistry.

Artistry is the creation of art. Creativity is simply the ability to create. As human beings, we are all creating every second of every day. When you think of where to go for lunch, you created a thought. When you come with an idea for how to surprise your family or friends with a gift, you are creating an idea. When you think about where you want to be in 5 years, you are being creative.

Therefore, since you are creating all the time, it makes sense that the more powerful your creativity is, the more powerful you will be.

The Key to Self Confidence

Feeling creative is the first step towards being self-confident. Self-confidence comes from feeling like you are in control; that no matter what happens you will be able to handle it.

Some people increase their self-confidence by sticking to situations with which they are 100% comfortable. Always going to the same stores, same restaurants, same areas. They hang out with the same people, stay at the same job, and never try anything new. In those environments, they are extremely self-confident.

The challenge is that once pushed out of those areas, for any reason, their self-confidence plummets. A better way is to realize that you have the capability to handle most anything that comes your way. If you believe you are immensely creative, then you accept that no matter what happens you will be able to tap your creativity and handle it. The key to confidence is not thinking through every situation that might possibly happen. The key is to get to a point where you trust in your own ability to think quickly, be creative, and flow with whatever happens.

You Can Solve Problems

The fundamental "real-world" application of creativity is problem-solving. Everyone has problems. No matter how hard we try to avoid them, problems will creep into our lives. The more creative you are, the better able you will be to solve those problems.

Here's an interesting thing about problems: the solution to a problem has to lie outside of your current awareness. If the solution lay inside what you are currently aware of, then you would know the solution and you wouldn't have the problem! Therefore, to solve your problems you need to tap that amazing creative power *"The more powerful your creativity is, the more powerful you will be."* you have. Many people don't realize this and choose to just live with the problem hoping that it will go away. Or they try to force solutions onto problems that just don't fit (the "square peg in a round hole" syndrome).

What's nice about unleashing your creativity is that problems will stress you out less. If you believe and trust in your ability to

111

create solutions, then when a problem arises you will not get overly stressed. Rather, you will realize that you will figure it out. Even if you have no idea how right now, you will be comfortable in the fact that you will figure it out.

Innovate New Ideas

When you are tapping your creativity innovation becomes a real possibility. Innovation is creating a new idea or enhancing an existing one. Innovation is vital in the business world. Companies are constantly looking for an "edge," such as a new service or product that will set them apart from the competition. By tapping your creativity you open yourself up to originating those ideas.

Innovation is not just useful in a business sense. We all get into routines and ruts in our lives. Innovating is a great way to make sure that our relationships, hobbies, activities, and lives in general stay fresh.

This Ties to Self-Expression

Creativity ties into the section on self-expression. When you are being creative, you are truly expressing who you are (you'll see why when we talk about how to be creative).

The idea of the tortured artist "expressing himself" through his work is clichéd, but there is some truth in it. Creativity is not about being clever and witty; it's about creating ideas that come from inside of you and are true to you. The more you let your creativity flow, the more you will be expressing yourself and the more satisfied you will be.

Stop Thinking, Start Flowing

The first step in tapping into your creativity is gaining an understanding of where it comes from.

Think of two parts of the mind: the conscious and the subconscious. The conscious is the part that thinks. It's the part that you are aware of. The subconscious handles everything else. Your bodily functions, sensory input, memories, feelings, associations, and more are all handled by the subconscious.

The subconscious is much more powerful than the conscious. The subconscious handles thousands of things every minute. The conscious mind can only focus on one. Even when you think you multi-task, you are actually switching your focus very quickly among different things, and it is your subconscious that is handling everything else.

The real power of creativity lies in the subconscious. Your creativity comes out of all the things you are not aware of – memories you don't remember, things you have seen but have not noticed, and feelings within you that naturally occur. All of your new great ideas are lying inside of your subconscious, right now. The trick is in figuring out how to access them.

The answer is *not* by **thinking**. Once you start to think, you are back to the conscious. When you use your conscious mind, you are only going to come up with one or two ideas. These ideas will not yield that great 'aha!' moment that you're looking for. In addition, thinking and using the conscious mind blocks your ability to access your subconscious.

The Metaphor of the Pond

In order to really access your subconscious, you must make your mind quiet and still. This is the only way to allow the subconscious to work, and it is the only way you will be able to hear what your mind is telling you.

Here's a metaphor that might make it easier to understand:

Think of a pond. Now, imagine throwing a pebble into the pond. If the pond is still and calm, the pebble creates clearly visible ripples. If the pond is turbulent when the pebble goes in, any ripples the pebble might make are hidden amongst the churning waters.

Your mind is like the pond. When you are calm and your mind is quiet, it is like the still pond. The pebble is a question or problem you have. When you pose this question to your still mind, your subconscious creates possible answers. These answers are the ripples on the water. When your mind is calm, you can actually 'see' all the solutions your mind is giving you.

On the other hand, if your mind is going wild with thoughts and stress, it is like the turbulent pond. When you throw in the question or problem, even if your mind comes up with answers, you will never be able to see them for all the turbulence.

In the chapter "Staying in the Moment" above, we talked about 3 ways of letting go of thoughts: meditation, journaling, and silence. Practicing those techniques will also help you quiet your mind when you are being creative, which will help you really tap into your subconscious. Make your mind like the quiet pond, and you will find yourself really coming up with powerful solutions and ideas.

The key is to develop a flow. That is, you have to let ideas flow from your subconscious out of your brain. The challenge in doing this is that the conscious mind sits between you and your subconscious, and the conscious mind loves to cut off that "creative flow."

Filters

A very common question I have been asked as an improviser is, "What if you can't think of anything to say?" The simple answer to that question is that it never happens. This is not because I am such a superb performer, but rather that I know how the mind works. I know that the issue is never that I have nothing to say. The issue is that I can't think of anything to say *that I think is good enough.*

As humans, we tend to watch our words carefully, and be very critical of what we say before we say it. As a society, we instill this behavior from a very young age. Young children are told by their parents, "Don't say that! Don't do that!" Then the kids go off to school and teachers tell them, "Don't do that! Don't say that!" Then the child makes friends and needs to be wary of what he says for fear that his friends and classmates will make fun of him. As the child grows and goes to high school and college, the concept of "political correctness" is introduced. Then he gets a job, and workplace sensitivity and harassment issues make him watch his words even more closely.

To a degree, these limitations are positive. It is a good thing to create a work environment where no one feels offended by anyone else's remarks. In terms of creativity, however, these limitations, or filters, create people who are unwilling to express and explore their inner ideas.

The best approach is to be aware of your filters and have control of them. The filter to avoid saying something offensive at work is a good one that benefits you. The filter that stops you from saying something stupid may be useful, but it also may be set too high. You might be afraid of expressing a good idea because you fear someone will make fun of you for it. Have you ever been in the situation where you had a thought but didn't say anything, and then two minutes later someone else says the same thing and is applauded for it?

When it comes to tapping into your subconscious and letting your creativity flow, filters are deadly. They are the primary reason most people who could otherwise be creative feel that they are not. When you are being creative, and especially when you are first practicing to tap into your creativity, you must get rid of these filters all together. Later on, you can start adding them back in, but only after you have developed the skill to let your creativity flow.

Bypass Your Filters

Once you have quieted your mind and started accessing your subconscious thoughts, your creativity will naturally develop. Unfortunately, right around this time your conscious mind will rear its ugly head (Ok, maybe your conscious mind doesn't have an "ugly" head, but when it comes to being creative, your conscious will hold you back).

As ideas are generated your filters will kick in. To truly unleash your creativity you have to bypass those filters. Here are a few ways to do that:

1. Go Fast

The first method to get around your filters is speed. It is possible to go so fast that you bypass the conscious mind and go right into the subconscious.

If you are generating ideas out loud, just say them – blurt them out. And keep blurting them out as fast as you can. This will open the door to new creative ideas.

Similarly, if you are writing ideas out then keep the pen moving. Don't pause, because when you pause you are stopping to think, and that cuts off your creative flow.

You have to trust yourself - you have to start talking and let the ideas come from inside of you and let them flow out of you without stopping. This means you have to create a "safe" environment, especially at first. If you are with a group of people, everyone has to know the ground rules so that you feel comfortable to go fast and say things. You also have to give yourself permission to let whatever comes out come out, regardless of what it might be.

You'll know you're doing it right, whatever creative thing you're doing, when you surprise yourself, because then your ears and your mind are hearing things at the same time.

2. Don't Evaluate

The second key to bypassing filters is to commit to a "no evaluation" policy.

When you start flowing, your subconscious will give you some crazy ideas, most of which won't be any good. The point at this stage is not to come up with a great idea, but rather to simply get your creativity flowing. This means that you have to be willing to say (or write) ideas that are bad, stupid, silly, or impossible. This is the way flow works. You may have an idea that is bad. That idea may lead your mind to think of another idea which is also bad. That second idea may spark a third idea which is ok, and that may lead to an idea which is actually good. If you stop to evaluate as you go however, you will be cutting off your flow after the first idea. This means that you would never get anywhere near that good idea.

Not evaluating requires commitment. It requires your commitment not to criticize or block any idea that comes up, no matter how inane. It also requires the commitment of everyone you are working with not to criticize an idea, and to just use the ideas as fodder for new ideas. The evaluation process can and should happen later.

Distract the Mind

A useful technique to unleash your creative prowess is to distract the mind.

I am sure you have had the situation where you were thinking about a problem as hard as you could, but no solution was coming to you. Then, hours later, after you had stopped thinking about it and while you were doing something else, you got a brilliant solution. This is how the subconscious works. If you put your conscious mind on something, your subconscious can't work on it.

Where do you get your best ideas? In the shower? While on a walk? For me it's while driving or while shooting baskets. No one has ever answered that question, "while sitting at my desk staring at my computer screen." And yet this is what most people do when confronted with a challenge (especially a work challenge). Try distracting your conscious mind by doing something unrelated and let you subconscious chew on it for a while. You may be impressed with the results.

Ask Yourself Questions

Sometimes people have trouble being creative because they have not properly phrased the questions they want their creative minds to answer.

I was doing a session with some high-level executives once and I asked, "What is one of the biggest challenges you are currently facing?" The answer came back, "The franchises!" to which everyone laughed and agreed. I wanted them to be more specific, so I asked, "What's the problem with the franchises?" The answer? "They are the problem!"

I tried to rephrase the question one or two more times to get them to be specific about the issue, but to no avail. They just stared at me as if the answer was obvious. Of course, if it was so obvious, why couldn't they state it? I was tempted to go into a lengthy explanation of creativity and how it relates to strategic planning, but that wasn't the point of the session, so we moved on.

Both the conscious and subconscious work by answering questions. They will answer any question you pose (in the pond metaphor, the question is like the pebble you are throwing in). The better the question, the better the response you will receive. And yet many of us are like those executives who felt it was enough to "just know" as opposed to being able to articulate the challenges.

For example, people may say, "I need to get in shape." or "I want to make more money." or, "I hate my job." To really unleash your creative potential, you need to rephrase these as specific questions that your mind can wrap itself around:

> "How can I lose 15 pounds in a way that I will enjoy and stick to?"
> "What can I do to earn an additional $10,000 a year without going crazy?"
> "What steps can I take to enjoy my current job more? or,
> "How can I get a better job doing what I love that pays more and that I will enjoy?"

Be sure to be clear in what you are after. If you can not be clear in your question, how can you expect your mind to be clear in its answer?

Be curious

A great way to stimulate your creativity is to get curious. Too often people walk around the world and look at things that are different and think of them as weird or wrong. Or they don't think about them at all.

Ask yourself things like, "Why is that the way it is?" "How did this come about?" (not in a negative way, but in a curious way), or "How did this person get to where he is?" Your subconscious mind will start wrapping itself around these questions and start thinking in new directions.

In addition to spurring on your creativity, being curious is a great way to shift your attitude from a feeling of being overwhelmed and in

"Being curious is a great way to shift your attitude from a feeling of being overwhelmed and in despair to feeling positive and in control."

despair to feeling positive and in control. When a problem arises, instead of being angry, get curious about the problem. "I wonder what caused this?", "Why is this happening?" (again, asked with curiosity, not with negativity!).

This will instantly shift your focus from how bad things are to understanding the problem and finding solutions.

Remember That Creativity is a Discipline

Creativity is a habit and a discipline. Don't be misled by the myth of the "creative genius." Chances are that most of the people you would consider to be "creative" have a fair amount of discipline in their lives.

The music virtuoso spent years studying and practicing. The brilliant painter spent hundreds and thousands of hours working on the canvas. The prolific writer has thousands of pages of writing that will never be published.

Do some people find the skills and habits of creativity easier than others? Yes. Does that mean that creativity is not for everyone? No. The primary key to success with creativity (and any endeavor) is to keep at it. Practice the exercises over and over. Keep applying the principles until they get easier and easier.

There is one distinction between people who excel and people who "don't get it." Those who excel try to do the best they can and they always seek to improve. Those who don't improve just go through the motions of the exercises and then get frustrated when nothing works for them. Practice doesn't make perfect. Practice makes permanent. If you go through the motions without really applying the principles, you will never learn. If you do exercises and drills without trying your best or seeking to improve, you will stay at the same level you have been. When doing your own exercises, make sure to do more than just go through the motions.

Remember, to get free access to over 25 exercises and improv games to help practice these principles, visit **www.AvishParashar.com/bookbonus**

Principle #8:

Trust Yourself

Improv is an exercise in trust. You trust the audience will like what you do and will not be mean (and not heckle). You trust your fellow performers to support you on stage. But most of all, you have to trust yourself that no matter what happens you will be able to handle it and flow.

To succeed at anything new in your life, you have to have this same level of trust in yourself. Until you display the level of trust in yourself, you will be hesitant and not be able to throw yourself fully into your activity.

Why this is important

When you trust yourself, you get a few benefits:

1. You Can Relax

People who are stressed do not trust themselves. Oh, they may act with a tremendous amount of bravado and bluster, and they may complain about everything else, but the underlying cause of their stress is that they don't trust themselves.

If you trust yourself, then you eliminate the need to stress. Once you believe that you can handle anything, you can start to really sit back and relax.

2. You Can Try New Things

The primary reason people don't try new things is the fear of failure. The primary cause of the fear of failure is that on some level, people don't believe they can handle it. Whether it's rejection, embarrassment, or loss, if you don't trust that you can live with the worst case scenario, you will be too paralyzed to take action.

3. You Can Do Better

As in the previous chapters on focus and fear, when you trust in yourself you can stop focusing on potentially bad outcomes and stop worrying about messing up. You can then put all of your attention on the task and hand, and therefore do it much better.

Improvisers who don't trust themselves won't excel on stage. In the same way, people who don't trust themselves in life won't succeed.

How Do You Develop Trust?

Obviously, the more experienced you are at something and the better you are at something, the more you will trust yourself. This goes back to the chapter on being willing to fail (over and over!). Take small steps, be willing to mess it up, and watch yourself quickly improve.

However, this approach won't work for everything. Also, you can't prepare for and practice every scenario, so it is important to develop an overall sense of self-trust instead of just a situation specific sense. The mentality you want is, "No matter what happens, I know I can handle it."

Remember Your Mind Gave You the 1st Thing For a Reason

The first level self-trust is to trust all those ideas that pop into your head when you are thinking creatively. Too often, people ignore their instincts or inner voice because they immediately discard what comes from inside of them. The mind is a powerful thing. If a thought is coming up from inside of you it is coming up for a reason. Don't ignore or discard it. Pay attention to it and remember that it came up for a reason.

This doesn't mean that you have to be stupid. If your mind is telling you to quit your job and move to the woods, that doesn't mean that you should storm into your boss's office this second and quit! Rather it means that instead of saying, "That's a stupid idea," say "Hmmm, I wonder what that's all about." (Remember the bit on curiosity in the creativity chapter?) That thought may mean that you need to get a different job, or restructure your current one. It may just mean that you need to alter or change how you spend your weekends and evenings. It could mean that you do need to quit and move to the woods, but you should think it through and get your ducks in a row before you do so.

Your subconscious mind stores memories, feelings, associations, dreams, desires, and more. If you have a thought, especially a persistent thought, trust in yourself and give it some credence.

Believe You Can Handle Anything (But Again, Don't Be Stupid)

To be a self-trusting person, start with the belief that you can handle anything. When a new situation arises, what is your first thought? Are you an, "I don't know about that," person, or a "Bring it on!" type of person?

In improv comedy, the distinction between these two types of people becomes quickly apparent when it comes to taking audience suggestions. Audiences often like to yell particularly different and crazy suggestions. Some improvisers hate getting really out of the box suggestions, while others relish it. As you may have guessed, I fall into the "relishing it" side of things.

This is not to say that crazy suggestions always made for better improv. In fact, often times a basic suggestion ("kitchen") created a much better scene than a crazy one, ("inside a crater on the planet Jupiter"). I relished the out-of-the-box suggestions and pushed people to do the same because of the underlying mentality you must have to do so. I could care less what suggestion I get because I trust myself to be able to do something with it. Most times I see people shying away from the crazy way it is because they are not comfortable with it. They will create other reasons ("Those suggestions are stupid," or "The audience doesn't like that."), but underneath, it comes down to trust and comfort.

Believing you can handle anything doesn't mean you act stupid. I have a background in martial arts. I believe I can handle myself in a fight if I have to. That doesn't mean I am going to walk in bad neighborhoods in the middle of the night or start throwing my weight around in a bar.

Believing you can handle anything is really a way of looking at life. It's realizing that nothing happens without challenges, and the more you can relish those challenges, the faster you will proceed.

Ideas are Infinite

Ideas are infinite. Accept that premise, and you will be set for life, in improv or business. Don't accept that premise, and you doom yourself to a bleak future.

Okay, maybe that was a bit excessive, but the truth is that if you do not believe there is an infinite number of ideas out there, you will have trouble with this whole trust thing. Why is this? Well, let's assume that you believe that ideas are *not* infinite. You believe that there are only so many good ideas (or solutions, campaigns, designs, etc.). That means that if you come up with a good idea, you believe you have grabbed one of the few good ones out there. You will therefore hold onto that idea because you can't be certain if there's another one anywhere.

Unfortunately, something will come along to make your idea invalid or not so good. Without the belief in infinite ideas, this will throw you because you will be holding on to your own idea. This seems implausible. You may be thinking, "Well, of course I would change my idea if something came along to make it not so good." It sounds obvious, but we examples of it everyday. The person who stays in a bad relationship because he doesn't want to deal with finding a new one is a perfect one. The executive who turns a blind eye to the changing market because he is so fond of his current product idea.

"Nothing happens without challenges, and the more you can relish those challenges, the faster you will proceed."

How does this relate to trust? Not believing in infinite ideas is what creates the "round peg in a square hole" syndrome. Rather than letting go of an idea and saying, "I trust that I will come up with something as good or better," you say, "I have a good solution. Let me apply it to everything!"

This is less about fact and more about *belief.* No one can prove whether ideas are infinite. You either choose to believe it or not. I like to believe that they are infinite. I like to believe that no matter how good my current idea is, I could come up with a new one that is as good or better. This attitude will allow you to believe that every problem has a solution, which is a very powerful belief to have when it comes to business and life. The opposite approach, that ideas are limited, restricts people's power and willingness to push forward and try new things.

In the absence of real proof, always go for the more empowering alternative. In this case that alternative is that ideas are infinite and that you can tap into them when needed.

Trusting Others

Self-trust is the key to trusting others. In my experience as an improviser and actor, I have played a variety of trust exercises. As a director, I stopped using them years ago.

If you are not familiar with trust exercises, they involve putting people into situations where they have to trust each other. For example, one member may stand with his back to the group, and then fall backwards, trusting

"In the absence of real proof, always go for the more empowering alternative."

the others to catch him. When they do, his level of trust for the group increases. Or so the theory goes...

My issue with most of these trust exercises is that they hope to translate trust in one area to another. That is, they assume that just because I trust you to not let me physically hurt myself that that means that I should trust you to respect my ideas in the work place. I have enough faith in humanity to believe that most mature people, even strangers, would not let me fall and hurt myself. I also have enough of an understanding of people to know that many just don't know how to listen and work together effectively. Trust in one area does not necessarily translate to the other area.

In order for you to trust someone else in a specific venue (such as in the workplace), one of two things needs to happen. First, you could spend a lot of time working with her. You would eventually learn her capabilities and develop a relationship that you understood and trusted. This is fine, and this is the way most trust is built, but it also takes a long time. This also leads to a situation where you force others to prove their trustworthiness to you, so you don't trust people when you first meet them.

The second way for you to trust someone else is to have enough confidence in your own abilities to take a chance and go ahead and trust them. A primary reason you don't trust others is that you are afraid of how their letting you down will impact your life. If you trust someone to complete a project on time and he doesn't, you could be in trouble with your boss. If you trust a person to respect and listen to your ideas and he doesn't, you may feel bad or embarrassed. If you have faith in your own abilities though, then you have faith that if someone does let you down you will be able to deal with it. This relieves a tremendous amount of pressure, and actually allows you to open up and trust people you don't know well.

This doesn't mean you should be naïve. If you do have a big project and are working with someone you don't know, you should trust him. But you should also stay on top of the situation. Weigh the risks and then decide. However, in many cases if you believe in yourself, you will be able to give others the benefit of the doubt.

Remember, to get free access to over 25 exercises and improv games to help practice these principles, visit ***www.AvishParashar.com/bookbonus***

Principle #9:

Exude Confidence

One of my favorite sayings when teaching improv comedy is, "The audience will appreciate you more if you confidently mess up than if you tentatively succeed."

An audience can sense when an improviser is tentative or hesitant. He may end up doing everything correct technically when it comes to improvising, but that hesitation keeps him from connecting with the audience. On the flip side, a performer can do many, many things wrong, but if she does it with gusto and confidence, an audience will give her all the support on the world.

This is not to say that it's a good idea to mess up and that you should ignore the rules. One of the most annoying traits a person can have, whether as an improviser or elsewhere, is to repeatedly and flagrantly do things wrong and not care because he is getting a good response (In show biz, this is called "pandering.").

The point of the rule "fail with confidence" is to get people to realize that confidence can compensate for so much. Confidence is an absolutely critical component of success in any arena. If you are not confident, you may stumble into success, but you will never be able to go out and grab life by the horns and get all you want.

People who are successful are confident. Don't make the mistake of assuming that they are confident because they are successful. The reverse is true: they are successful because they are confident. If you were able to take a look at them before they achieved their success, they would still look extremely confident.

If you could make only one mental shift in your life, I would say that approaching every situation from a place of 100% confidence would be the shift that would help you attain your goals more quickly and easily.

Insecurity is rampant in our world. It's not all or nothing. Most people are confident in some areas and insecure in others. The key is to make sure that you have confidence in the areas that really matter.

Think about the areas in your life in which you are not as successful as you would like to be. Chances are, you lack confidence in those areas. Here are a few ways to start approaching life with confidence:

Believe In Your Own Infinite Potential

In the previous chapter, we talked about ideas being infinite and trusting in yourself. Those beliefs are the first step down the road towards confidence.

To take it one step further, you have to believe in your own infinite potential. Believe that you can do anything, handle anything, and solve anything, and your confidence will go up. This idea is just an extension of creativity and self-trust. If you have been working on tapping your creativity and practicing the ideas around trusting yourself, then you should already feel your confidence building.

Get Out of Your Own Way

Most people think their lack of confidence comes from outside of them; "I don't know how they will react.", "I don't know what will happen."

In truth, the lack of confidence comes from inside their own heads. Most of us are constantly getting in our own way. We psych ourselves out, have long dialogs with ourselves about why we will fail, and create elaborate movies of our impending failure in our minds.

We all also procrastinate, do things we know we shouldn't, make bad choices, and put off doing what's important. All of these things come from inside. To truly succeed, you have to get out of your own way. Stop being negative, stop conjuring up destructive images, and stop bad mouthing yourself in your own mind!

The first step in doing this is to catch yourself when it happens. Pay attention, catch yourself, and then commit to changing your approach. Just like we covered in the chapter on focus, when you find yourself getting in your own way, shift your focus to what you want, to the positive potential, and tune your inner dialog to a more positive station.

Embrace Uncertainty

The single biggest destroyer of confidence is uncertainty. Consider a situation where you feel very confident. It's most likely a situation where you are pretty certain of what is going to happen and what other people are going to do.

On the flip side are the situations where you are not confident. These situations are usually wrought with these types of uncertainty: "What are they going to say? What are they going to do? What's going to happen now?"

One way to deal with this is to follow the advice given above. Condition yourself and your creativity so you feel ready to handle anything.

Another way is to get to a point where you **embrace uncertainty**. Rather than being stressed about the unknown, start to view it as a wonderful opportunity. To do that, you must really take a look at uncertainty. What is it and what causes it? Certainty comes from the familiar. The more familiar you are with something, the more certain you are as to what's going to happen. Even in improv comedy, when you play the same games over and over you get a sense of certainty because you know how well they will go and how the audience will react.

"Rather than being stressed about the unknown, start to view it as a wonderful opportunity."

Once something becomes familiar, it enters your comfort zone. You encounter it so much that you become comfortable with it. By extension, this means that things that are outside of our comfort zone are unfamiliar and uncertain.

This is exactly why embracing uncertainty is so important! All of your growth, progress, innovation, and success lie just outside your comfort zone. Why is that? Because if they were already in your comfort zone you would already have them!

Start looking at uncertainty as an opportunity to get out of your comfort zone and grow as an individual. Once you look at it that way, your confidence will go up in situations in which you used to be totally uncertain.

Fake it Until You Make It

Most people believe that confidence comes from the inside out. That is, first you feel confident on the inside and then you start acting confident on the outside. This is absolutely true, but it is not the only way it can work.

If you pretend to be confident on the outside, you will soon find your inner confidence growing. Take on the mannerisms of confidence. Stand up straight with good posture. Look up, smile, and make eye contact with people. Talk slowly (not too slow, but don't race over your words) and speak with a steady voice.

This is what it means to "fake it until you make it." Pretend to be confident on the outside by doing all of the above. When you do, you will actually find your inner confidence growing by leaps and bounds. By forcing yourself to act confident, you will eventually get to a point where the confidence happens without your pretending. You will have "made it!"

Remember, confidence is a vital attitude to have. It is the often forgotten key to success. A little bit of skill and a lot of confidence can and will take you a very, very long way. Just imagine what a lot of skill and a lot of confidence could do!

Remember, to get free access to over 25 exercises and improv games to help practice these principles, visit **www.AvishParashar.com/bookbonus**

Principle #10:

Hocus Focus!

Focus is an important concept in improv and life. Too often we all have an inability to manage our focus. This leads us to get distracted, get off path, ruin our mood, and be much less effective than we could be. One of the primary ways that people limit their effectiveness is by putting their focus and attention in the wrong place.

What You Focus On is What You Get

Quite simply put, what you focus on is what you get. We have already talked about how negative people put their focus on negative things, and positive people tend to focus on positive things; however, your focus controls more than just your attitude. The choices you make regarding what you focus on have a huge impact on your success and productivity.

You are drawn to what you focus on. You've probably had the experience of buying a new car or piece of clothing, and then when you are out you see that same car or clothing item everywhere. You probably have no recollection of seeing it before, but now you see it everywhere. Did the car or clothing suddenly start appearing after you bought it? No, of course not; they were always out there, but when you weren't focusing on them you didn't "see" them. After you bought your own, you started to focus on it, and then duplicates started "appearing" in your life.

As mentioned earlier, if you focus on negatives, you will find negatives. If you focus on positives, you will find positives. If you focus on why something will be impossible, you will find more and more reasons that it can never be accomplished. If you focus on how great something will be or on what a great opportunity you have, more of those will show up to. Just by shifting your focus you can seemingly "attract" great things into your life – in truth they have always been there, you were just unable to see them before!

Increased Productivity

In addition to making you more aware of the opportunities in your life, controlling your focus is the key to maximizing your productivity. Every time management program talks about priorities. It may be setting your to-do lists into quadrants by identifying what's important and/or urgent, assigning priorities in an "A, B, C, D" fashion, or just starring the "musts" in your life. There's a reason each time management program talks about them because they are important!

By identifying what's important and then focusing on it, you are guaranteeing a huge boost to your productivity. When thinking about your day and life, consider the 80/20 rule: Eighty percent of your results will come from twenty percent of your activities. Most people spend their time focusing on eighty percent of the activities that only give twenty percent of the results.

Focus shifting such as this will allow you to get more done in far less time. More importantly, it will ensure that the highest priority tasks get done.

After having applied this idea of focus shifting into my own improv comedy performing and directing career, my improv really improved. In an improv game, there are hundreds of things to focus on. Most people tend to either try to focus on all of them or focus on the little things that seem important but really aren't critical.

Most improv games, like the ones you have seen throughout this book, have "rules." For the first few years I did improv I focused primarily on mastering those rules and playing the games "right." This is what most improvisers do. Then I realized that the rules themselves were not what gave the greatest results – they were the 80% that yielded 20% of the results (results in this case being the audience's response). The critical 20% which most people don't focus on was the underlying mentality. I realized that my focus had to be on making sure I was staying in the moment and working with my partners. I still did my best to play the "rules" right, but my focus went to the other two things. Not only did my performance improve immensely, but the other things, like the rules, fell into place easily.

That is the way life will work. Focus on the most important stuff, and the other stuff will fall into place. Even if it doesn't, it is not that important because the other stuff doesn't matter as much.

Think about your own life and work. What are the critical "20%" activities that net you the greatest results and reward? Put your focus on those activities, and you will get more done in less time and be more successful doing it.

Freeing Up Energy

Imagine that you are a big ball of energy. (Actually, since physics has shown us that matter and energy are the same thing, calling you a big ball of energy is neither incorrect nor insulting). The sum total of your energy can be divided amongst many things. It can also be tied up in your own being. Your goal, if you want to perform at a maximum level, should be to free up as much of your energy as possible.

This ties into focus because your focus can either be in or out. You direct your energy through your focus. When you are angry, depressed, or worried, your focus is internal. You have an inordinate amount of energy tied up in how you feel. When you are happy, laughing, and positive, your focus is external. Not only is none of your energy tied up in yourself, but also you generate more energy through your emotions.

Think about your body when you are filled with a negative emotion. Typically, your muscles tense up, your body contracts, and your head is down. What do all these things point to? Tense muscles means you are using energy to tense them. A contracted body requires energy to keep it contracted. And what are you doing with your head down? You are reflective, focusing on things inside your own head. All of these things use up energy that could better be used elsewhere.

"Your goal, if you want to perform at a maximum level, should be to free up as much of your energy as possible."

Now, think about when you are positive. What is your body doing then? The body in these cases is usually loose, pumped up, and your posture is good: straight back, head up, and eyes out. In these positive times, you are projecting energy out to the world. You are not tying up energy in tension, and you are focused on all he things going on around you.

Can you recall a time where you were feeling pretty average, or even a bit down, and then suddenly you received a piece of great news? What happened to you? Did you stay slumped in your chair, feeling pretty average? I'm going to go out on a limb and say "No way!" You probably got really jazzed, and wanted to run out and tell someone about it. You may have found it hard to sit in one place, when just moments before you were content to lie around. That's positive focus (focusing on the new, great news) generating energy for you!

This is true in many different ways-- positive vs. negative, solutions vs. problems, etc.. The distinction that is rarely talked about though is whether your focus is internal or external. Simply, most people focus internally when they should be external, and focus externally when they should be internal. As a quick definition, when I say internal focus I mean the idea of paying attention to your own thoughts, being caught up with your own inner dialog, and putting pressure on yourself. External focus is paying attention to others, keeping on open mind, and looking outside of "you" for help.

Having an Internal Focus When It Should Be External

Most people spend an inordinate amount of time in their own heads. Pay attention to yourself for the next 24 hours. How often are you wrapped up in your own thoughts and inner dialog? This is fine most of the time, but notice how often you do that when you should be outside of your own head. For example, when someone is talking to you, do you listen completely, or do you immediately start thinking of other things (your response, why they are wrong, what you need to do later that day, what happened at an earlier meeting? This is a classic case of having an internal focus when you should be external.

In order to have a relationship (professional or personal), you need to interact with other people. To have a strong relationship, you need to put more of your focus on the other person and pay attention to them.

I would be so bold as to say that 90% of communication problems can be attributed to people focusing internally when they should be external.

Having an External Focus when it Should be Internal

On the flip side, most people also tend to think externally when they should think internally. For example, when something goes wrong, where does your focus go? Do you try to find out who messed up and blame them? Do you look immediately for a new tool, skill, or person to help you? These solutions aren't bad, but you should first turn internally.

Rather than immediately looking outside of yourself, look inward and ask, "How can I use this?" Or, "what result do I want?" Or, "what can I do?"

This response will serve two purposes. First, it will marshal your resources to start thinking of solutions, instead of dwelling on the problem. Second, it will increase your team cohesion because instead of looking for fault, you will be working with people to solve issues.

By focusing internally, I don't mean blaming yourself. I mean believing that the solution is within you, and looking inside to find the solution. The next time you feel overwhelmed, upset, or stressed, take a moment and notice whether your focus is internal or external. Then try switching it, and see what a difference a new perspective makes.

How to Control Your Focus

The best way to control your focus is to pay attention to what's going on in your mind. Our inner thoughts control our focus. The best way to control those inner thoughts is to examine the questions you are asking yourself. When your mind is faced with a question, whether it is posed by yourself or someone else, your focus goes to the analysis of the question. Your mind can't help but try to answer it.

If you are walking around asking yourself, "What could go wrong?' or "What are all the reasons why this won't work?" Guess where your focus is going? If instead, you ask yourself, "How can I make this work?" Or, "What can I do to ensure success?" Then your focus will go to the positives.

For prioritization, ask yourself, "Which one thing if I accomplished would have the greatest positive impact on my life?" That simple question can instantly help you isolate the critical 20% activities for anything-- just replace "life" with "job," "relationship," or whatever area you are focusing on. It seems simple and it is. It just takes practice, especially if your habit is to focus in the wrong place.

Remember, to get free access to over 25 exercises and improv games to help practice these principles, visit **www.AvishParashar.com/bookbonus**

Principle #11:

Get Your Body Into It

Before any improv show the performers will warm-up. Improv warm ups consist of games that get some blood flowing, sharpen the mind, and get everybody focused. In my beginning years as a director, I would run warm-up exercises that required a certain degree of skill, and often (especially when energy was low or people were unfocused) the skill warm-ups would not go well. Then we would stop and discuss and reinforce the skill.

The problem was that the 20 minutes right before a show is the wrong time to try to teach anything. Sure, you can remind people of things they need to remember, but by playing skill games and then critiquing, I was filling people's heads with extra things to think about.

I switched over to doing warm-ups that did nothing but energize everyone and get people laughing. I threw out all the skill exercises and warmed up just with fun energizers. I realized that the goal of improv warm-ups wasn't to get people ready to do improv, but rather to *get their heads in a place where they could do the best improv possible.* This may seem like a very small difference, but it made a huge difference. The shows became more fun, the quality went up, and things started flowing smoother.

Every warm up had some element of energizing. The key was to get the blood flowing. Your results off the improv stage will absolutely come the same way. If you try to tackle something when your energy is low, you will get low results. If you energize and get the blood flowing, you will be able to attack things which much more vigor and success.

Think about a time when a problem was "weighing you down." What were your energy and body like in that situation? Did you feel ready to tackle that problem? Of course not. Now think about a time when you felt good about something. How were your energy and body at that point? You probably felt ready to tackle the world!

There is no reason to wait for something good to happen externally to improve your energy. You can take control of your body, increase your energy, and then be able to succeed at a much more rapid pace.

Get Energized, More Productive, and More Effective

To be more effective and productive, consider energizing before you start your own work. You don't have to jump up and down and sing songs like an improv performer, but you do want to get your blood flowing and get some focus.

If you happen to have your own office with a door you can close, feel free to move around and jump up and down. If you work in a cubicle or in an office where people can see you, you don't have to act like a madman. But even doing something as simple as stretching, breathing deep, or taking a walk can help you out.

Many people exercise first thing in the morning or on their lunch break. This is an excellent way to start the day right or re-energize in the middle of the day. Should you get your blood flowing every time before working on anything? In an ideal world yes – that will ratchet up your productivity in everything that you do. However, if that seems excessive, then start small.

Firstly, make sure to energize when you are feeling "down." If you sit down in front of the computer screen and feel slumped, then take two minutes to energize. At first it will feel like you are wasting time, but two minutes now will save you much more than that in increased productivity.

Secondly, I would highly recommend energizing before doing anything creative. If you are going to sit and enter data, then maybe you don't need the blood flowing. However, if you are going to write, or brainstorm ideas, or anything where you need to tap your creativity, then definitely make sure your energy is up.

Finally, if you find yourself distracted or if you are finding it hard to concentrate, then taking a brief break to get some blood flowing will be immensely helpful.

Exercise

Obviously the best way to energize is to exercise. Whether it's walking, jogging, playing a sport, lifting weights, or anything else that gets the blood flowing, exercise will increase your productivity and creativity. While it's not always practical to run off to the gym for an hour, you can do little things to break your mood and get the blood going. The simplest is to take a walk.

Stretching

One thing you can do, even in a cubicle, is to stretch. Stand up, stretch your arms, and twist around. Sometimes we sit in front of our desks for so long we forget to get up. We also don't realize just how stiff we are getting. Take a few minutes every hour or so to stand up and stretch around to get the blood flowing.

Posture

Bad posture really contracts your body which contracts your energy. Put yourself in the right posture and that helps your breathing and lets you access those positive resources and get the creative juices flowing.

Here are some signs of negative and positive posture:

Negative	Positive
Body hunched over	Body up tall
Unhealthy 'C' shaped curve to spine	Healthy 'S' shaped curve to spine
Head Down	Head Up
Eyes down	Eyes straight ahead or up
Frowning	Smiling
Shoulders slumped	Shoulders slightly back

Try it now. Try hunching over and contracting your body. How positive and creative do you feel? Now sit up straight with your head up and chest slightly out. How does that feel? By simply adjusting your posture you can shift your energy and increase your productivity.

Breathing

One of the fastest ways to martial your resources and center yourself is to control your breathing. Most people breathe very shallow; that is, when they breathe, they only fill the top part of their lungs. Try breathing in deeply, to a point where your belly actually expands because it is filling with air. This may takes some practice, but after a while it will become very natural.

In addition to being very good for you, this style of breathing will calm your mind, improve your focus, and get your creative mind ready to go. This technique is especially great if you are starting to feel overwhelmed. Take a few controlled deep breathes to calm yourself and focus, and then use your creativity to make a plan to get out from under (I will discuss exactly how to do that later in the book).

You should also be using this style of breathing to improve your meditation. When you meditate (you are meditating, right?), if you find it difficult to clear your mind, try just focusing on breathing properly. This will improve your breathing and keep your mind from over-thinking.

Smile

There's not a whole lot of exercise involved in smiling, yet that one physical act can cause an instant shift in your energy and mood. Try it right now. Put a big smile on your face. You will immediately feel better and you should feel a small but noticeable shift in your energy.

This is a great technique to use anytime, anywhere. Most people forget to smile anyway. Keep reminding yourself to smile – it will make you feel better and will probably influence the people around you too.

Remember, to get free access to over 25 exercises and improv games to help practice these principles, visit
www.AvishParashar.com/bookbonus

Principle #12:

Kick Yourself Out Of Your Comfort Zone

One of the great things about teaching improvisational comedy is that I get to see people stretch themselves and do things they never thought possible. For most people, improv comedy is out of their comfort zone. Watching a person step out of their comfort zone and gradually (or sometimes even rapidly) expand their comfort zone is a wonderful thing. This concept applies to much more than just improv comedy. Getting out of your comfort zone is vital to any kind of success and to your own development.

All success lies outside of your comfort zone

Here's an important fact that most people never think about: unless you are 100% satisfied with everything in your life, you must get out of your comfort zone!

To rephrase that: if there is any area of your life where you are not getting the success you want and deserve, you have to get out of your comfort zone to get it.

There is a quote that sums up why this is true. "If you keep doing what you've always done then you'll keep getting what you've always gotten." If what you've always gotten (and are currently getting) is not what you want, then you need to do something different. Unfortunately, "different" is usually outside of our comfort zone. If you could just do what you were already comfortable with to achieve your success, you'd already be doing it.

The problem is that we don't like getting out of our comfort zones. The word "comfort" is used deliberately. That means that getting out of your comfort zone is "uncomfortable." Naturally, we don't like to be uncomfortable.

The mentality that keeps us in our comfort zone is subtle though, and often comes up in the form of avoidance. That is, we don't say, "I could have what I want, it's just that it's outside of my comfort zone." Instead we blame externalities, "If people would just hire me then my business would be successful," or we limit ourselves, "Oh, I could never do that." In the worst case, we ignore it all together. We don't think about what we want or could have, and we refuse to talk about. It remains a dream buried deep down in the back of our heads for years (regrettably, sometimes forever).

In my years of doing improvisational comedy, I hear the same suggestions over and over (audiences love to yell, "bathroom" for a location and "spatula" for an object – don't ask me why!). There is a strong temptation to "re-use" old material. If I have done a joke or scene based on that suggestion previously, I may want to repeat it since I know it worked before. In fact, I have seen many; many improvisers go down this route. Re-doing on old scene is a classic "comfort zone" technique.

I learned early on however that a joke or scene never works as well the second time around. In improv, it's the act of doing something new (stepping out of the comfort zone) that increases the enjoyment and quality. Once it has been done and is comfortable, something is missing.

Life works the same way. Staying in the comfort zone feels safe and good, but the quality is never the same.

Are You in Mental Prison?

Staying in your comfort zone is a nice way to feel good, but your comfort zone can easily become your prison. People often fool themselves into believing that what they have is enough, or that they are satisfied with what they have achieved. This gets worse as more time goes on. The more you stay in your comfort zone, the harder it gets to break out. This is how people get "set in their ways" as they get older.

"Staying in the comfort zone feels safe and good, but the quality is never the same."

The more this happens, the more prison-like your comfort zone becomes. You start to ignore and avoid all those things you want because you know deep down that they are out of your comfort zone. This is not to say that should feel obligated to constantly strive for more. There are areas of your life where you life where you like what you have and are fine staying in your comfort zone. That's fine. You just have to be honest with yourself about your level of satisfaction

You Only Regret What You Don't Do

Regret can be a painful thing. If you feel regret it means that you acted in a way you wish you had not. Sometimes you regret a choice you made or a thoughtless comment you said. Most of our regrets, however, come in the form of things we didn't do. These are the regrets we feel when we stay in our comfort zone.

These regrets range from the large, the career path you didn't take; to the small, the show you wish you caught on Broadway; to the "who knows," the person you didn't introduce yourself to. These are the regrets that nag at you late at night. These are the ones that make your heart wistful when you see someone else doing what you have always wanted to. These regrets are your inner self's way of signaling you that you have to get out of your comfort zone.

Most people as they get later on in life and recount what they regret invariably list the things they didn't do: "I wish I had spent more time with my family." "I wish I had applied to art school." "I wish I saw more of the world." They probably don't even realize it, but the thing that kept them from doing those things was their comfort zone.

There is no substitute for action. The interesting thing is that if you regret something you did, you can fix it with an apology,

"No amount of practice, theory, advice, or role playing will expand your comfort zone the way actually doing it will."

or conversation, or by making amends. There is no way to fix something you didn't do. The opportunity is past, and all you can do is look for the next one. If you find yourself regretting things, remember – that's a signal telling you that you must get out of your comfort zone the next time the opportunity arises.

Preparation vs. Productivity

You can prepare to get out of your comfort zone, but never mistake that for productivity. Many people, myself included at times, keep preparing to grow. We read and research, take classes, get advice, and talk to people ad infinitum about what we are going to do. While a certain amount of preparation is a good thing, excessive planning is just a brilliantly subtle way for you to stay in your comfort zone. What you are trying to do is to expand your comfort zone with knowledge, theory and advice, hoping that you will expand your comfort zone without actually doing anything.

Guess what? No amount of practice, theory, advice, or role playing will expand your comfort zone the way actually doing it will. The world is unpredictable. Even if you practice a situation one hundred times in your head, you will still have to get out and do it and chances are it will somehow go different than you expected.

I once heard someone say, "An ounce of implementation is worth a pound of theory." I agree. Do get out of and expand your comfort zone, get out and try. Don't fool yourself by 'over-preparation."

Think "Yes And"

The key to getting out of your comfort zone is to switch your thinking from "yes, but" to "yes, and."

"Yes, but" is a default mentality that most people have that keeps them in their comfort zones. When someone comes to them with a new idea or opportunity, their first reaction is to say, "yes, but..." Whatever follows the "but" is why they won't take the action and therefore not get out of their comfort zone.

"Yes, and" is a much more powerful mentality that leads to progress and growth. When presented with a new idea or opportunity, a "yes, and" person reacts by saying, "yes, and..." Whatever follows the "and" is why they will take action or what else they could do with that opportunity. Switching from "Yes, but," to "Yes, and," is the fastest way to adjust your mentality to force you out of your comfort zone and onto progress.

You probably say "yes but" quite a bit. Even if you don't use the exact words "yes, but" you probably say it in spirit. This is not indictment – it's completely natural. As stated above, it's a lot easier to stay in your comfort zone. But that doesn't make it right. The worst "buts" are when you "but" yourself. You probably have lots of thoughts and ideas of things you could and should do, but as soon as the idea pops up you hear a little voice in your head saying, "but…"

This ties directly into our regrets. When you regret something you didn't do, your mind told you do it but then you said, "but." Later on, you regret it because you know that you should have…

The first step here is to start catching yourself saying "but." Pay attention and notice how many times you say it, literally or in spirit. The next step is to start to switch the "but" to an "and."

I Can't Say "Yes, And" to Everything!

You are correct. Adopting a "yes, and" mentality doesn't mean that you agree with everything that comes along. Sometimes people are going to give recommendations that you are legitimately bad, and once in while you'll have an idea that you shouldn't follow. "yes, and" is not about blind acceptance or optimism. It is a way of changing your initial reaction.

When an idea comes up, *first* think "yes, and." This allows you to explore the idea and keep an open mind. After properly thinking it through you can decide whether you want to follow through or not. When you immediately say "but," you end the thought process. By first saying "and" you not only think about it but also increase your motivation. When you say "yes, and" you think about what benefits you will get by taking action and also what else you could do. This increases your likelihood of doing the right thing.

In the worst case, by saying "yes, and" you will force yourself to be honest with yourself. If you start out saying "yes, and," then if you ultimately decide to not take action, you will know whether it is because it is legitimately a bad idea or if you are staying in your comfort zone. "Yes and" is also a cornerstone communication idea which we will get to in the chapter on communication.

Step Off the Ledge

One of my favorite expressions to get myself to do things and take chances is, "step off the ledge."

I love movies, and I am a big fan of the Indiana Jones trilogy. In the third installment, *Indiana Jones and the Last Crusade*, Indiana Jones needs to pass a large chasm in his quest for the Holy Grail. He is standing at the edge of a cliff, and the other side is much to far to jump. His only clue is a picture of a knight floating in air towards the grail.

Meanwhile, his father is lying some distance away. He is actually the Grail expert, but he has been shot. He knows that secret and keeps repeating, "you have to believe boy." Finally, Indiana Jones has a realization, and, without any evidence, he takes a big step off the ledge. Miraculously, he doesn't fall to his death, but rather, a bridge appears to support him.

Yes, this is just a movie, and no, I am not advocating that you go to a high cliff and take a big step off. However, I am advocating that you approach the metaphorical cliff in your mind and "step off the ledge." Like Indiana Jones, most people's reluctance to taking a big step like that is their lack of faith.

"What if I do this and I fail? What if I get rejected? What if I mess up?" To really succeed at something you must have faith that it will work out and just "step of the ledge." This is not a license to be stupid. If you have no savings, I am not saying you should quit your job today and try to make it as an actor, if that's your dream (although there are some out there who would).

Having faith and stepping off the ledge is about realizing that there are no guarantees in life, and nothing will ever be perfect. Ultimately, to succeed, you have to commit yourself 100% and have faith. In improv comedy, this may be the single biggest thing that holds back performers. Rather than jumping in to an exercise with gusto they stay timid, or try to stay vague, or act as if they would rather be somewhere else. With this approach, they will never make it.

This also leads to an unfortunate cycle. They are timid, so they don't do as well, so they don't get a great response from the audience. This of course undermines their confidence, which makes them more timid, which hurts their performance, and so on. Once you commit and have faith, things begin happening and rolling. Until that point, you are just playing around.

Take the 1st Step and Start!

The key to getting out of your comfort zone is to just take one step. Too often, we all stop ourselves because we feel we need to make some grand gesture or "do it all." When I teach improvisers, new or experienced, there are usually hundreds of things I could be correcting them on. I prefer to pick one or two specific ideas and focus only on those. I actually let them do other things wrong without correcting them.

This only works if I do two things. 1) I make sure that what I am focusing on is more important than what I am ignoring 2) I let them know that I am only focusing on one thing so that they realize that just because I am not correcting something doesn't mean it is correct.

I do this because to correct everything at once would be giving the improviser too much to think about. How can anyone comfortably perform improv if they are thinking of 100 different things. I prefer to take it one step at a time, focusing on one critical piece at a time.

The Japanese call this principle Kaizen, which basically means small incremental improvements (Literally, it means "change for the better" or "improvement"). Too often, we try to fix everything all at once and do things perfectly on our first try. I know when I wanted to jump into cold calling I tried to commit to one hour a day of dialing numbers. One hour a day! I hated 5 minutes of it and I was trying to force myself to do it for 12 times that long!

The only time I really stayed consistent with the calls was when I committed to dialing the phone 5 times per day. Some days I would do more, but all I had to do was 5. This was enough to get me started. Soon I had completed 500!

When you are trying to get sales and you are only dialing the phone 5 times a day, it seems incredibly inefficient and a sure path to failure. But, if you set your goal so high that you bail out, that's an even surer path to failure. We live in an immediate gratification kind of world. When we want something, all too often we launch out with huge aspirations and take massive action, but all too often that effort lasts about a day or two and then we are right back where we started.

Getting out of your comfort zone works the same way. If you take little steps that net little results, you will eventually make big progress. The problem is when you either a) try to bite off too much at once and then lose confidence because it doesn't work or b) don't acknowledge all the little steps because they seem so small and insignificant. Make your tasks small, but still forward moving, and give yourself credit for even the tiniest progress. Soon you will build new habits that will have expanded your comfort zone immensely.

10% Good Enough

Sometimes all you need is just a little step. In improv, a performer who tries to figure out exactly what he is going to do in advance will be hopelessly overwhelmed. Moreover, he will be lost if something arises that doesn't quite go along with his idea. The performer's best bet is to go strongly with whatever idea comes up with, even if it is not fully formed. As the performance continues, the performer's own creativity will flesh out the idea as it goes.

In the same way, rather than trying to do everything all at once, a person should just get started. When you start, it gives you something to build off of and learn from. Will every start develop into something great? Of course not, but 100% of the times you don't start will go nowhere. "You miss 100% of the shots you don't take" – Wayne Gretzky.

In the martial arts, when two people are fighting, one person does not have to be twice as good as the other to win. In fact, a person doesn't even need to be a better fighter overall to win; he just needs to be a better fighter at the right moment. Even then, he doesn't need to be a lot better in one moment; he *"If you take little steps that net little results, you will eventually make big progress."* need be only ten percent better in one moment to win the fight. This is true if the fighter knows how to leverage that ten percent. You see, a fighter doesn't need to win the fight with one punch – he just needs to use the 1/10 of a second that his opponent is stunned to land a second punch, and then use that opening to land a third, and so on and so on. In this way, the fighter leverages a 10% advantage into a 100% victory.

The fighter leverages a 10% advantage into a 100% victory. By taking small steps and continuously building off of them, you too can turn little steps into big success.

Leap Before You look (But Be Smart)

No, that's not a typo. The traditional adage is in fact, "look before you leap," which is a fine cautionary saying about knowing what you are getting yourself into. In improv however, I teach people to do the reverse-- to "leap before you look."

In an improv sense, this works masterfully. Many performers get into the habit of trying to plan out everything they are going to do in an improv scene right from the get go. This results in two problems. First, it's hard to come up with an entire scene's worth of material up front, so they don't do well. Second, because of the nature of the form, many things can happen that makes it impossible for the performer to stick to his plan.

When you leap before you look, you just start performing and focus on what you are doing in the moment. You figure out where you are going and how you are going to get there as you go. 90% of the time this results in a great funny scene. The important thing to remember with this concept is that it is not reckless. It just puts goals and risk into perspective and then demands action. With an improv performance, the goal is to entertain, and the only risk is that the audience will not enjoy the show. With those two parameters, the concept of leaping before you look makes a lot of sense.

Beyond the stage, it takes a little more refining. I am not advocating that you quit your job and become a writer (if that's your dream) without getting your ducks in a row. You have responsibilities and need to assess the risks and chances for success. I am advocating that you do not worry about having every last detail planned out before you start. As with improv, life will throw you curveballs that will invalidate even the best plans. Get the big picture set, make sure that you have a strong desire, have a plan, and then start.

In 1961 President John F. Kennedy said, "I believe that this nation should commit itself to achieving the goal, before this decade is out, of landing a man on the Moon and returning him safely to the Earth." At the time, no one knew how they would do it. But the goal was set, so they figured out how. In 1969 Neil

Armstrong became the first man to walk on the moon and safely return.

"Leap before you look," is just a way to remind yourself that the timing will never be exactly right. The critical thing is that you get started and commit. There are few things in personal development scarier than kicking yourself out of your comfort zone. Once you embrace the concept however, you will find yourself doing and achieving more than you thought possible.

Remember, to get free access to over 25 exercises and improv games to help practice these principles, visit **www.AvishParashar.com/bookbonus**

Principle #13:

Shut Up and Listen

Up to now, we have been focusing on things that you can pretty much handle on your own. If you do everything in the book up to this point you will do quite well. The challenging part of the world, however, is that there are other people in it. No, I am not being cynical. But it doesn't matter how well you can express yourself or creative you are if you can't interact effectively with other people.

The first step to effective interaction is to shut up and listen! There are books, classes, and entire courses devoted to communication, and yet most of them focus on how to speak or convey your point clearly. These courses unfortunately miss half the equation. Listening, not talking, should be the first focus of communication.

In improv comedy, listening is critical. Since you have no opportunity to confer or pre-plan, you must work with other performers to make up a scene as you go along. The only way to do this is for all the performers to really listen to each other. Unfortunately, I see countless scenes where one or all of the players aren't listening. They all have their ideas of what they want to do or so, and when one person says something the others barely acknowledge it and push through with their own ideas. The result is always bad improv.

The world unfortunately works the same way. Rather than spending time listening to each other, most people get too caught up in their own thoughts and ideas and try to push ahead with them. We all get too caught up in trying to tell people things – trying to show them what we know; trying to convince them we are right. We would all get a lot further in our relationships if we changed our focus to listening first and speaking second.

If you need a trite reminder of this just remember that you have 2 ears and one mouth. Try to follow that ratio and you should be fine.

Real Listening

Right now, you may be confused. "But Avish, I listen– I have been listening my whole life!" Simply using your ears is not real listening. Most people engage in what I call "fake listening." When someone is talking, you give them half of your attention but your mind is elsewhere. Maybe you are thinking of something that happened earlier in the day or something that you have to do later. Or perhaps they said something that made your mind wander away.

If it's an argument, it's quite possible that once they have said five words you already know what you are going to say back. You've long since stopped listening; now you are just waiting for your turn to speak! Real listening is when you empty your mind and put your attention 100% on them. Just like in creativity, the key to success here is to empty your mind.

So what exactly is an "empty mind?" When I talk about having an empty mind during workshops and seminars, people usually don't know what I am talking about (occasionally someone will joke about certain politicians having empty minds...). Having an empty mind does not mean that a person should sit there staring vacuously into space. Rather, it means having the ultimate open mind. Similar to an empty cup (see Principle #6) waiting to receive water, the mind should be in a state where it is ready to receive input.

In order for you to keep a properly empty mind, you must push all extraneous thoughts out. If you are speaking to someone then you must focus on what they are saying. You must not think about the meeting you have coming up, the project you have to do, or the fight you just had with a friend.

You must also ignore the impulse to start formulating an answer before the other person is finished. Focus on what they are saying, not on what you want to say. Similarly, push aside what you think you already know. If someone is talking to you about a problem they are having and you have had a similar problem in your life, resist the urge to start thinking that you know all about their problem. Every situation is different and sometimes what you think you know can have as strong negative consequences as what you don't know. I'm not saying you can't use your experience to help them-- that's probably why they came to you in the first place. What I am saying is that you need to listen and wait for them to finish before you start comparing it to your past. You may find that the situations are not entirely identical.

Having a truly empty mind means staying in the moment. Don't think ahead to what is coming up or what you will say, and don't think behind to past experiences. Just be in the moment and watch your creativity and communication skills go through the roof.

Pay Attention to the Other Person

The simplest, fastest, and best way to work with someone and make them feel valued is to *pay attention to them*. Sound too simple? Well, read on! I have seen it hundreds of time on stage. An improviser has so much to worry about– his character, the set (which is usually imaginary, so he needs to keep track of it in his head), how to be funny, the rules of the game, the audience, etc.–

that he quickly forgets to pay attention to the other performers on stage. Even though the other performers are the only help he has, they are the first to go out of his mind. This results in disjointed and unfunny improv.

This same situation occurs off the stage. Have you ever been talking to somebody at a party? Do you focus entirely on the person you are speaking with or does your attention keep jumping around the room to all the other people there. Generally, if the person is someone you really want to talk to (a good friend, key business contact, potential relationship, etc) you will focus on them. Most other people will only get about half of your attention.

You may think that this is ok, because if you don't really want to talk to them then what does it matter if you don't give them your full attention? Consider two things. First, you may just not realize the benefit of that conversation. If you are at a networking meeting and you hope to meet the CEO of Company X but you end up talking to someone who has a low-level job at a different company, then you may let your attention wander as you speak to him. But maybe you don't realize that this person has already met the CEO and could introduce you. Do you think he will do that if he feels you don't really care about speaking to him? This doesn't mean you need to spend the entire time talking to him. Five or ten minutes of real attentive conversation can be worth 30 minutes to an hour of partial attention interaction.

Second, whether you want to speak to someone changes based on the situation. You can love your spouse, but if he or she tries to talk to you while you are watching something you like on TV, where is your attention going? Make your own decision, but if you want them to feel valued, give them your full attention. The nice thing is that in many cases you can give them your attention for a few minutes and then return to what you were doing. You miss very little, they feel valued, and all is well.

The first step is awareness. Next time you are talking to somebody, try to see where your attention is going. If it's not on them, get it back!

Active Listening

This is a good time to talk about "active listening." Active listening is a technique whereby you do many little things to listen effectively. These can range from positioning your body in a certain way to controlling how you are looking at the person to subtly repeating things they say. There are many, many things you can do to "actively listen."

On the surface, active listening sounds great. In reality, I think it's just too complicated! If you have to remember dozens of little things to do, one of two things is going to happen. 1) You will not do any of them because you will get overwhelmed. 2) You will be so caught up in your head "thinking" of all the things to do that you won't be able to really listen at all.

"If you simply empty your mind and put your attention on the other person, you will find yourself naturally doing the active listening techniques."

If you simply empty your mind and put your attention on the other person, you will find yourself naturally doing the active listening techniques. Your body will position properly, your gaze will go the right place, and you will repeat and comment when it is natural. Don't worry about the active listening – just empty your mind and focus on the other person.

Self Confidence and Self-Control

One of the main obstacles to real listening is our own desire to speak and be heard. This desire comes from a few places:

1) You Are Right and They Are Wrong!

Of course you are...

We have all been in an argument where the other person says something that is just flat out wrong. This always triggers an immediate need to break in and point out why they are wrong. What usually happens at this point? The other person gets even angrier because you interrupted them. On top of that, they probably believe that they are right and you are wrong, so they get even angrier at your stupidity!

It is important for you to keep your goal in mind in these scenarios. Is it your goal to get mad and make the other person mad? I certainly hope not (I have come across people who really enjoy getting others mad, and I can truly say I don't like those people!) Regardless of if your goal is to defuse the situation or to win the argument, not listening and interrupting are not going to help you.

You must have the self-control to refrain from speaking and continue to listen. File away what they said – you can address it in a few minutes when they are done. For now, keep listening. This will reduce the tension and also make them feel that you are listening.

If you find it hard to do this it may be because you lack self-confidence. You are afraid that by not speaking up immediately the other person will take your silence for agreement. That is not true at all, as long as you calmly state your response after they have finished!. Also, your resistance may come from fear that if you don't say something now that you will miss the opportunity or forget. This comes from the scarcity mentality. If what you have to say is so important you will remember it. If you don't remember it, your mind will give you something else.

2) Significance and Connection

I have been in the following situation many times. See if it sounds familiar to you.

I do improv comedy and professional speaking. Both are relatively uncommon fields, and when you combine them it's unique. Oftentimes when I meet new people we go over the typical pleasantries of "What do you do?" When I explain it, I would say that at least 50% of the time the person will say, "Oh, I do that," or "My brother does comedy." Okay, they don't always say "brother," but they will point out either themselves or someone they know who does comedy.

What does this do? I'll tell you what it does – it takes the wind out of my sails! Think about it: a few seconds ago we were talking about me, and now we're talking about somebody else – often a person not even in the same room! I'm sure I sound egotistical here, wanting the conversation to be about me. But remember what Dale Carnegie said, "You can make more friends in two months by becoming more interested in other people than you can in two years by trying to get people interested in you."

If you want to make friends or just make some connections, be interested in them. Don't force the conversation around to you or people you know! It's not easy…I'm on the other side of it quite a bit as well. My best friend is a musician and composer. When I encounter people in music I feel that, "Oh, my best friend is a composer," statement welling up inside of me. I have gotten much better about not saying it, but it is hard.

The desire to chime in like that does not come from a malicious place. It comes from our desire to either be significant or form a connection. Sometimes we want to feel important. If somebody says something they do that is an accomplishment you don't want to be left out. I train in the martial arts and have a second degree black belt. When I meet someone who has been training for a couple of years and they say so (usually with a certain amount of passion and pride) I feel a strong urge to "drop in" that I too train and have more than one black belt. That's just my ego chiming in.

It's amazing though – the other person has not said a single thing to diminish my accomplishment, but I feel if I don't say that I too train that I have somehow been diminished. If you really want to see this in action go watch parents interact with other parents of kids the same age. It's an incredible game of one-upmanship!

Going back to the earlier chapters, if you are tapping into and expressing your true self, your sense of self-worth comes from within, not from how you compare to others. Once you realize that, your need to chime in will reduce. Of course, the desire to interrupt and say "me too!" may come from a desire for connection, not significance. As humans, we all like to be connected to other people, and one way to achieve that connection is

"You will connect much faster by being interested in someone than by telling them how great you are."

commonalities. So when someone says that they achieve something that you too achieved, you want to chime in to create a connection.

The motive isn't bad, but it's counterproductive. Remember, you will connect much faster by being interested in someone than by telling them how great you are. Does this mean that if you have something in common with someone that you shouldn't say so? No, of course not. The point here is to not interrupt someone else, and not try to one up them. Conversations have a natural flow. There will be an appropriate time for you to say, "me too," or "I have a cousin who also..." When that thought rises, file it away and use it for conversation later. For now, keep listening, keep your attention on the other person, and make them important.

3) Thoughtlessness

Sometimes when we interrupt there's no underlying motive at all. We're just being thoughtless. This kind of interruption comes from two places: either you weren't paying attention or the person overstayed their welcome.

If you don't pay good attention than you will indeed thoughtlessly interrupt. You've seen it happen many times, I'm sure. Someone (maybe you) is talking, and then someone else (hopefully not you) interrupts with a question or comment unrelated to what's going on. It's incredibly rude, and it's fixable by applying the simple listening skills above.

Sometimes, unfortunately, people abuse your good listening skills. They talk on and on about things that you have no interest in. In this case, interrupting isn't thoughtless (though it may seem so to the other person) – it's survival! Interrupt away, get out, and move on to someone else who has more respect for your listening skills!

Real listening is the key to solid relationships. If you listen properly you will get three key benefits:

You Will Start to Pay Attention to All the Things You Would Have Otherwise Missed

I'm sure you've been in the situation before: You are talking to a friend, and they say something that triggers a thought or memory. Your mind drifts, but your friend keeps talking. At the end of what he says, he says something interesting, but you have missed everything leading up to it. You then have to either pretend you have been paying attention and fake it or say, "I'm sorry, could you repeat that."

In a casual conversation with a friend, this is no big deal. But if you are in an in-depth discussion with someone you care about, or even on a sales call, those little things that you miss might be the key to the conversation. In those situations it is also incredibly awkward and embarrassing to have to ask the other person to repeat himself.

For example, imagine that you are having a "discussion" with your significant other. She starts to say that she is hurt that you were out late last night. You may immediately get defensive and feel the need to jump in and argue about how you are entitled to have some fun and don't need to answer to her and are feeling stifled, etc. If you control that urge and just listen, she may go on to say that she's ok with you going out, but she would appreciate a call so she doesn't worry. This would change the entire tone of the conversation, and keep you out of a fight.

You Can Understand Tone and Body Language

People's bodies and voices often tell us a lot more about what is going on in their heads than the actual words they use. If you get wrapped up in your own thoughts, you can not pay attention to the subtle signals they are sending. If, on the other hand, you empty your mind and put 100% of your attention on the other person, your mind will be completely open to these signals. These signals will tell you if a person if interested, bored, or beginning to get angry. It will also clue you in as to whether they are telling you the entire story – often people will be holding back but you won't know it unless you catch their tone and body.

This is a huge communication tool! Having the ability to discern whether or not a person is holding back will greatly improve your ability to connect with them. In personal relationships, you'll know whether your partner means it when he says, "I'm fine." In sales, you'll be sure if a prospect really doesn't have the money or is hiding a deeper reason to not hire you. In business, you'll be able to serve your customers and co-workers better by discovering what they really want.

Diffusing Situations

As mentioned above, real listening is the key to reducing the conflict in your life. Most fights can be avoided long before they start. If you are paying attention, you will know when someone is starting to get irritated. You can take the steps at that point to shift to discussion to avoid a fight.

Also, oftentimes people don't need you to do exactly what they are saying. While they would of course like it, they don't need it. What they do need is to feel like you have listened to them and treated them with respect. Real listening accomplishes that. Letting your mind wander or especially interrupting them shows that you are not listening and not respecting them.

This is How to Get Rapport

If you employ this level of real listening, you will find yourself developing fast rapport with people. In this world, so few people really pay attention that you will stand out. Think of the person that you know that you consider very "empathic." The person you feel you can talk to about anything. I'm guessing that they are already naturally employing this style of listening.

When you listen like this you are also making the other person the most important person in that moment– that's a sure way to develop rapport with people! This idea of really listening sounds simple, and it is. At the same time, it will be difficult to do at first, but keep practicing– it is the single most powerful thing you can do to improve your communication and relationships!

Remember, to get free access to over 25 exercises and improv games to help practice these principles, visit
www.AvishParashar.com/bookbonus

Principle #14:

Let Go of Control

Being on an improv stage can be a very scary thing. You have nothing prepared in advance, you have an audience just waiting to laugh (or not!), and you have other performers who will have their own ideas about what to do. Many improvisers, especially new ones, will feel a great deal of stress wondering what their partners are going to do. Well meaning performers will get wrapped up in their own thoughts trying to figure out what's in their partner's head so they can help support them. Non-well meaning (or just oblivious) performers will stress that their partner won't support them or that their partner will do something stupid or crazy.

I was like this too for a while, until I came to a great, if obvious, conclusion: the only thing I could control on that stage was my choice of actions. Ergo, there was no point in worrying about what my partner might do. Whatever he did, I would flow with it. The day I came to that conclusion is the day that my performance really took off. All the energy and focus I had previously been putting on stress, fear, and trying to "figure out" my fellow performers suddenly went to staying in the moment, paying attention, and doing the best I could with whatever was given to me.

The world works the same way. We all want to exert some level of control over all the things going on around us. This is a natural feeling, but if you give in to it you will really be reducing your ability to do well. Most of the disappointment, anger, and frustration people feel is when they do or say something and expect something specific to happen. When that thing doesn't happen, their desire for control kicks in and they get all out of whack.

The universe is tricky. No matter how well you plan, it's going to throw something unexpected at you. People are also unpredictable. You may clearly expect them to act in one way, but chances are they will do something else. The more you hold on to your desire to have them do things, "your way" the more stress and challenge you will face. This is not to say that you shouldn't have certain expectations. Just realize that all you can control is yourself; say what you need to, do what you need to, and expect a specific response. When that response doesn't come, just be prepared to let go, flow, and react to it the best you can.

This is the real key to dealing with change: realizing that the unexpected will occur, but realize that when it happens you will deal with it.

The Key to De-Stressing

Realizing that the only thing in the world you can truly control is yourself is the key to letting go of a lot of stress in your life. Think about the person you know who is the most "stressed out." Chances are that he's the person who feels the greatest need to control things around him. Things have to be a certain way, and if they are not they are "wrong" and must be fixed. He probably gets apoplectic when someone does something outside of his current belief of how things should be done.

Stress comes from either being upset at the way things are or from being worried about what "might" happen. Both of these are futile endeavors that are key examples that you are holding onto control.

The present is the way it is. No amount of anger or railing can change things as they are at this instant. You can take action to change things for the future, but things are now as they are. You can't control it. The more you get angry about the present, the more useless stress you will give yourself.

Similarly, the future is unknown. Things may or may not happen a certain way, and no amount of your focus will change it. Taking action right now may, but simply focusing and stressing over the future won't change anything. When you feel stress about the future, you are in a way trying to control the future by thinking about it: "I hope I get this job," "I hope the party goes well," "I hope my boss doesn't criticize me." Thinking about those things won't change them, but it will add to your stress.

> "The more you get angry about the present, the more useless stress you will give yourself."

Exert More Control by Letting Go

The great irony is that the more you focus on the one thing you can control-- yourself, the more impact you will have on the things you can't! The more focus you put on things you can't control (how someone messed up, what might happen, how someone else will respond, etc) the less focus you have to put onto the task at hand.

The key is to shift your focus off of all those things and back on to the one thing you can control: what you can do in this moment. Imagine that you have a big presentation coming up, and your mind is focusing on many things – how it will go, how the boss will respond, whether people will like it, whether they will be mean to you, etc. That kind of focus is doing nothing for you. In fact, too much thinking like that will paralyze you.

When those thoughts come up, shift your focus onto what you can control: working on the presentation right now. By putting your focus on that, you are doing all you an to make the presentation the best it possibly can be. Once you do this, the likelihood of your presentation being well received goes up. Therefore, the more you put your focus on what you can control, the more control you exert over everything else.

This focus shift is a great way to increase your productivity as well. When we put our focus on things outside of our control, we work slower, procrastinate more, and get easily distracted. Just when we start getting into it, our minds drift back to our stress and lose our flow.

By constantly reminding yourself that the only way to make a difference is to take the actions you can take right now, you will continue to work and make huge progress in less time than ever.

The key here is to catch yourself whenever your mind floats to the past, present, or onto something outside of yourself. Realize that those thoughts aren't serving you, and bring it back to what you can do right now.

We all know people who complain and stress but never do anything:

- The person who complains, "I'm fat," but never exercises and continues to eat poorly

- The person who whines, "I hate my boss," but never looks for a transfer or new job

- The person who stresses, "I hope that I pass my test," instead of studying!

For most people, putting focus on things outside of their control is natural. Don't fall into that trap, and you will find your productivity increasing and your stress level decreasing. As we will see in the next chapter this is the key to working together with other people as well.

Remember, to get free access to over 25 exercises and improv games to help practice these principles, visit **www.AvishParashar.com/bookbonus**

Principle #15:

Teamwork

On an improv stage, as in life, no man is an island. We all need to work effectively with the people around us to achieve more and fulfill our potential. While sometimes is it seems easier to rely entirely on your own wits and abilities, you can only go so far solo.

Teamwork is vital. Whether you are on a literal "team," such as in sports or business, or you just have people in your life you interact with regularly, such as friends and loved ones, your ability to collaborate with others will determine how far you go.

Teamwork and working together are given a lot of lip service, but most ideas around teamwork miss the mark.

I have been to teambuilding events where a group of people are supposed to "work together" to achieve some common goal. I have found two big limitations to almost every event I have participated in or witnessed:

1) Success Requires Little Teamwork at All!

In many of these events, one strong "alpha" personality will take charge and start coordinating and dictating what should be done. At the same time, the more timid people drift into the background and don't contribute at all. A team is truly working well together when there is give and take and the team is leveraging everyone's strengths. Most "teams" in the world don't really do that.

2) The Teambuilding Event Doesn't Transfer Any Real Usable Skill Set

Some events are designed so that each person must contribute. Often, these events require everyone to do the exact same thing in rhythm together (for example, a team rowing event).

This kind of activity will train "coordination," which is not the same thing as teamwork. Any group can be forced to do something in unison. The instructor may be able to pull out teamwork lessons from such an exercise and explain how the only way to succeed was for everyone to work together.

People are all individuals though. Once this group returns to the work place they will have no external force making them work in unison. The coordination (or "teamwork") will go right out the window. In any case, forcing people to be the same in the name of teamwork goes entirely against everything in this book about expressing yourself and unleashing your potential. The strongest teams are the ones where everyone is leveraging their own strengths. The only way to do this is for each team member to express themselves while also allowing and helping everyone else to express themselves.

"The strongest teams are the ones where everyone is leveraging their own strengths."

Circle Metaphor

Perhaps you are in a situation where you feel you don't need others. Maybe you are far smarter than the people around you, and you can come up with better ideas then them. Maybe you are doing just fine on your own, and in fact, sometimes you feel you are "carrying" everyone else.

Here's the thing though: even if the people around you don't contribute directly, *they can help you be more powerful yourself.* Don't believe me? Try this metaphor out:

Imagine you are at the center of a circle. For each idea you come up with, make a dot a certain distance away from you. Because you are creating each idea yourself, the dots will all be at the same distance away from you. Make a circle connecting the dots around you, and you have your circle of influence. The better the ideas, the farther away the dots, the bigger the circle, and the more power you have:

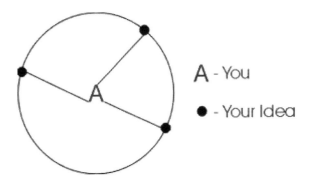

A - You

● - Your Idea

Now, imagine you are with a group of people, all of whom you are much smarter than. Every time you come up with an idea (a dot) someone in the group will riff off of that and generate a new idea (a new dot). Even if the idea is very weak and the dot is not that far away from the original, this gives you a new point to riff off:

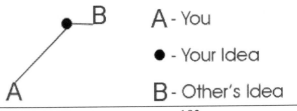

A - You

● - Your Idea

B - Other's Idea

You now have essentially doubled the size of your circle, as you have created a second set of ideas:

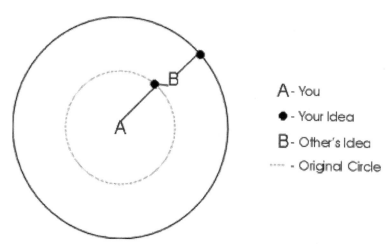

A - You

● - Your Idea

B - Other's Idea

···· - Original Circle

Without those other people, regardless of how great their ideas are, you would never have increased your own circle. Don't be so quick to write of the contribution of others – sometimes the benefit may be a little more subtle than you think.

As with everything else in improvisation, the key to a great team starts with a mental shift...

Mental Shift

To have a strong team, you need two things: 1) Strong individuals. 2) The right team mentality. The preceding chapters in this book are all about how to create strong individuals. Creating the right team mentality doesn't come from forcing people to work in unison, and it doesn't come from an artificial exercise. It comes from having everyone on the team thinking in proper way. The way to have a good team is to revisit the principles and mentalities from before and apply them to the team model.

Think "Yes, And"

As mentioned previously, thinking "Yes, and," is the best way to treat everyone with respect, listen to everyone's ideas, and keep the attitude inclusive. In the circle metaphor above, the ability to expand your own circle comes from your willingness to say "yes, and" to other people's ideas.

"Yes, but" not only stops people from accepting and expanding, but it also creates and incredibly negative atmosphere. When someone, or more than just one person, is "yes, butting" everything, it absolutely destroys teamwork.

Let Go of Control

Reminding yourself that the only thing you can control is yourself will foster a phenomenal sense of teamwork. Groups get undermined by people criticizing and critiquing each other, and also by stressing about what someone else is going to do.

Letting go of all of that and focusing on what you can control creates an atmosphere of trust. If I am not going to oversee and control everything you do, then I must on some level, trust you.

This is not to say that team members abandon each other and only focus on themselves. Quite the contrary, individuals focus not just on their own tasks and what they can control. However, if someone else messes up, they don't turn their back and say "I'm glad it wasn't me!" Instead, their thought process is "what can I do to make this better." Letting go also adds personal responsibility into a team. Rather than just focusing on their own tasks, individuals focus on what they can do to achieve the overall goal.

Both Give and Take

It is important that when you let go of control that you are willing to take it back. Most people have the problem of being unwilling to relinquish control– they try to micro-manage. A few others have the other problem; they never take control back and always take a back seat. The person who never takes initiative also undermines his team, just in a more subtle and passive way. Remember a good team is one where everyone is being themselves. If you are being passive and never taking initiative, how can you really be expressing yourself?

"If you are not contributing, then what purpose are you serving being on the team?"

While the controlling personalities usually run roughshod over everyone, they occasionally are right when they say, "no one else does anything." Make sure that you are both giving and taking control. Let others get their input and make them feel valued, but make sure you also get your input and ideas in. If you are not contributing, then what purpose are you serving being on the team?

Right Focus

More than anything else, the ability to shift your focus onto positive, forward moving ideas and off of negative and destructive ideas will help your team thrive.

Focus on Solutions Instead of Blame

When something goes wrong, what is your first instinct? What is your group's first instinct? Do you immediately start pointing fingers and assigning blame? Do you first make sure that someone else is implicated to make certain that blame can not come onto you? This is a common response, but it is a weak one. A much stronger response is to immediately put your focus on solutions. Instead of, "who's fault is this?" shift to "how can we fix this?"

This will serve two purposes. 1) You will solve the problem fast instead of dwelling on it. 2) By not blaming immediately you will not react right away in anger, which is a big team killer. Does this mean that you don't ever "blame?" No. It is very important that you identify what went wrong, and if applicable, who messed up. Then you have to address the person. If you don't do this, the problem (or a worse one) will happen again. The key is to shift your focus first on solutions, and second on blame. Most people (and most bad teams) do the reverse.

Focus On Getting Results Instead of Being Right

Most arguments are the result of two people desperately wanting to be right, and wanting the other person wanting to admit that they are right. Even if the debate starts logically enough, it usually devolves, especially once emotion and anger enter the picture. The problem is that when you get caught up in "being right" you are often taking actions that are moving you further and further away from getting what you really want.

I was teaching a class for a summer program on improvisation. One day, two girls in the back kept talking while I was explaining something. Finally, I asked one of them to move up and sit in the front. She refused saying, "I wasn't talking." I said that's fine, but could you please come sit up front. She started to argue. There happened to be administrators in the room to help with discipline, and they quickly acted and kicked her out of the room.

Once she left, I used this as an example for the rest of the class on being right versus getting a result. The fact was that I felt I was right– she and her friend had been talking throughout the class. She felt she was right– in that specific instance, maybe she wasn't the one who said something. She got caught up in arguing over being right that she lost sight of the result– to stay out of trouble and get through the program.

This happens all the time. When someone does or says something that we are 100% certain is wrong, something happens to our egos. We feel a huge need to rise up and make the other person acknowledge their error. In some cases I do agree that it is imperative to stand up for what is right. But those are big areas around integrity and character. Rosa Parks not giving up her seat on a bus is a social imperative. You ruining a nice dinner with your spouse because he didn't pick up the dry cleaning and won't admit that you told him to, even though you know you did, is not!

When you feel that sense of righteousness rising up, take a second and think it through. Is it worth the added aggravation and argument, and is it going to get you closer to where you want to go, or is it just going to sap energy from the important things in your life?

Positive Support

If you've spent more than a day in the corporate world, you've probably heard someone use the smarmy phrase, "We don't have problems; we have opportunities." I call that phrase smarmy not because I disagree with it, but because usually the person saying it is trying to puff out their chest and be a "good manager." Usually, they have no real idea what that phrase means.

In improv comedy, problems (or "mistakes") can often lead to some of the most brilliant performance, if the performers know how to flow with it. When something goes wrong, smart improvisers will acknowledge it, use it, and flow with it. Newer (or weaker) improvisers will get thrown by the mistake, freeze up, and then scramble to recover.

For example, one time my group was doing a show. Right as one game started, a person in the front row got up and walked right in front of the stage to go to the bathroom. I wasn't annoyed that he had to cross in front – it was the only way to go to the bathroom. What I (and my fellow performers) were annoyed at was that 1) he didn't have the sense to wait two minutes for a break between games, and 2) he didn't make any effort to duck or hurry therefore seeming as if he didn't even care.

Rather than get mad, frustrated, or thrown, my fellow performers and I suddenly shifted our game to focus on this person's rudeness. The guy was clearly on a date, so we shifted and made the scene an act-out of how his date was going (complete with rudely walking in front and going to the bathroom). The audience loved it, since they too knew he was rude, and the game ended up being one of the highlights of the performance (note: I normally never mock an audience member like that, but he deserved it and it was all in good fun).

When a problem happens, to really turn it into an opportunity you have to do a few things:

1) Acknowledge it

Too often people try to deal with a problem by ignoring or minimizing it.

2) Don't Get Angry

When the problem comes up, don't get angry or whine about how you wished this didn't happen. Keep your focus on what is happening right now.

3) Be Supportive

Create an atmosphere where everyone feels support, even the person who messed things up. You can deal with her later; for now, you may need her at her best to turn the problem around.

4) Use it

Ask yourself, "What can I do with this opportunity that I couldn't before?"

5) Do Not Seek to Return to the Status Quo

Most people's initial response to a problem is to try to get things back to the way they were before. This is the primary way in which even the most well intentioned people fail to turn problems into opportunities. When things get thrown out of whack in a crisis, don't ask, "How we can get things back to where they were?" but rather, "How we can make things even better than they were.

Do those five steps and you will really start to appreciate that challenges can be used to your advantage. Get your whole group on the same page, and you will really see the power of teamwork.

Remember, to get free access to over 25 exercises and improv games to help practice these principles, visit **www.AvishParashar.com/bookbonus**

Principle #16:

Communicate Clearly

Now that you have mastered everything else, we finally get to how to communicate your own points to other people. Why is this last? Because most people talk too much, listen too little, don't pay attention, and don't think! Also, most of the stuff we have covered so far applies when you are speaking as well.

In improv, clearly communicating your point is vital. If you have an idea on an improv stage, you must make sure to clearly convey it so that the other performers understand it. If you don't then they will have no idea what you are doing and go about working on their ideas.

This may even anger you – you might get mad at them for not supporting your ideas. However, if you don't communicate clearly, then the fault is your own. I have seen the following scenario (or a similar one) in improv more than I'd like to admit:

Two performers are acting out a scene. One person is playing the part of a "thief." When the other performer turns his back, the thief picks the other performer's pocket. The thief knows this, the audience sees it, *but the other performer has no way of knowing this happened!* When he turns back around, he will continue the scene oblivious to the pick-pocketing and therefore not support his partner's offer.

Similarly, I have seen performers be slick and throw out a vague offer only to have their partner miss it. Backstage, after the show, the one who made the offer will say, "When I said X, I wanted you to say Y." This is amazing. A performer makes an unclear offer and then blames the other person for essentially not being able to read their mind! Communication is the same way. We often get mad at others for not getting our message: "But I told you I wanted the blue one!" And yet we usually neglect to even consider that we probably have some responsibility for whether the communication was properly received.

The Meaning is the Message They Receive

A great phrase I heard long ago is "The meaning of the communication is the message they receive." Brilliant! What this means is that what you say and what you mean are irrelevant when it comes to communication. What really matters is what gets across! Too often we get caught up in "saying the words." We feel that if we just say what we need to say, that we have covered ourselves. Then, if and when the other person does something wrong, we blame them since we did our part.

This occurs in relationships all the time. How many couples which are on the path to divorce still say, "I love you" every day? The words aren't important; the meaning that the other person is getting is what's important.

In business, how often do people pass along memos and instructions without really paying deep attention to whether the meaning was properly conveyed? In the corporate world, priority number one is often to cover your own butt, so as long as you said what you had to you feel safe. You can later on always tell your boss, "Well I told Joan to do such and such!" This strategy will cover your butt, yet it will also hold your business back.

This style of miscommunication occurs very often in email. People write emails with a certain "tone of voice" in mind. As they right, they "hear" their own voice with inflections, emphasis, and sarcasm. They often forget that their voice does not get sent along with the email. Without the benefit of those inflections, emphasis, and sarcasm, the email may take on a totally different meaning. It is vital to think about the meaning your message will convey before sending something.

To make sure to communicate effectively, make sure to do the following:

Know Your Point

So simple, but so forgotten...

The most important thing when communicating is to know your point! To often people open their mouths and just start talking without knowing what the exact purpose of their communication is. How can you make sure that your message is getting across if you don't even know what the message is?

This level of communication is not vital if you are just shooting the breeze with friends, but if you are trying to convey something important, make sure you know what your point is. Take a few seconds before you speak to think it through. Most people are afraid of silence, but you will find that taking a few seconds won't throw off the conversation (the other person probably won't even notice) and it will improve your ability to get your message across.

Be Clear and Concise in What You Say

Even if you know the message you want to get across, you may still find yourself rambling. Rambling on and on is the enemy of good communication. When you state your point, say it directly and with as few words as possible.

Too often, especially when we are nervous or uncertain, we will continue to explain a point long after we should have stopped. This hurts our message in a few ways:

1) It Confuses the Issue

The more you talk the more chance you have of contradicting yourself or saying something confusing.

2) It Creates More Opportunities for Tangents

If you ramble on, your partner may address something in your rambling as opposed to the main point. All of sudden your discussing a completely different issue

"When you state your point, say it directly and with as few words as possible."

3) It Shuts Off Dialog

Real communication is a team game. When you ramble on what you are conveying is that you are so desperate to get your point across that you are insecure and don't want to hear what the other person has to say. If you make your point and get questions or comments back, you have a dialog going. That's a good thing!

4) You Can Lose the Listener

If you ramble, you give your partner the opportunity to zone out. Remember how hard "real listening" is? Now imagine someone who doesn't even know about real listening trying to follow you as you ramble on. Chances are you will lose them and they will completely miss your message.

Be clear and concise, and your point will get across.

Pay Attention

That's right – you have to pay attention to the other person when they speak, and you also have to pay attention to them when you speak! As you are speaking, notice what the other person is doing. How are their body language and facial expressions? What are they saying or doing in response. By paying attention to the other person, even as you are speaking, you can really see if the message you want to convey is getting across.

This gets to the heart of the matter: the point of your communication is not to say the words; it is to make sure the message gets across. Take your focus off the specific words and pay attention to whether they are getting the point, and your ability to communicate will quickly improve.

Speak From Their Perspective

If you were speaking to a five year old, you wouldn't use big terminology and speak in terms of big abstract theories. You would speak simply and use examples they could follow. You would be speaking from their perspective.

In the same way, when you speak to anyone, make sure you speak from their perspective, not yours.

Talk to any professional whose industry has profession-specific terminology, and you will see this in action. Doctors speak to patients with the highly technical jargon they use to talk to each other. Lawyers use legalese that the rest of us are clueless about. Even as a speaker and an improviser, I have to constantly remind myself that most people aren't familiar with basic improv terminology and concepts.

I was once meeting a potential client, and his directions told me to park in the "municipal lot" on a certain street. I didn't know exactly what that was, but I thought it would be self-evident once I got there. Big mistake! I turned onto the street and there was a large parking garage/lot on the right, so I pulled into there. That was the wrong place to go. I drove around the lot for 5 or 10 minutes then used my cell phone to figure out where I was actually supposed to be. Of course, when I did the client kept saying "municipal lot." Had he just said, "the small parking lot on the left side of the street," I would have found it no problem. I didn't know what that was, and he assumed I did. I am not blaming him; I should have asked. But this is a simple example of how we were both communicating from our own perspectives, and how that resulted in a miscommunication.

Speaking from the other person's perspective is just an extension of paying attention to them. When you put your attention on the other person, you will quickly understand what kind of language and terminology you should be using. The ability to communicate your point to others is vital. Take the time to pay attention, be concise, and speak form the other person's perspective and you will greatly reduce those annoying miscommunications that seem to always pop up.

Summing It All Up

There you have it. 16 simple but powerful ideas that will lead to success on or off the improv stage:

- **Principle #1: Have fun**

- **Principle #2: It's all in your head (get the right mindset)**

- **Principle #3: Express Yourself**

- **Principle #4: The only thing we have to fear**

- **Principle #5: Get out there and fail**

- **Principle #6: Stay in the moment**

- **Principle #7: Tap your creativity**

- **Principle #8: Trust Yourself**

- **Principle #9: Exude Confidence**

- **Principle #10: Hocus Focus!**

- **Principle #11: Get Your Body into It**

- **Principle #12: Kick Yourself Out of Your Comfort Zone**

- **Principle #13: Shut Up and Listen**

- **Principle #14: Let Go of Control**

- **Principle #15: Working Together**

- **Principle #16: Communicate Clearly**

It may seem a little overwhelming in that there's a lot to think about. Don't forget one of the primary improv comedy rules – don't think! Or at least, don't over think! Take it one piece at a time. The content is laid out so that sections build off of preceding ones. Start with the first principle and build off of that.

Just take it at your pace, play the games, practice the techniques, be willing to mess it up, and always, always, always remember to have fun!

Thanks for reading – and keep on improvising!

Avish Parashar

Get What You Want With Improv

Avish Parashar helps people and organizations get what they want through the art and science of improv. If you want to bring Avish to your business, association, conference, or event, contact him now. Everything Avish does uses improv, and organizations most commonly bring him to use improv to address one or more of the following areas:

Motivation – Avish's motivational, humorous, and interactive speeches are the perfect way to open or close an event or conference. In a short period of time, your group will be energized, entertained, and ready to apply the art and science of improv to their personal and professional lives.

Communication – In speech, breakout, or workshop form, Avish will address key communication issues your organization faces. These communication ideas can be applied to a variety of targeted areas, including teambuilding, customer service, and supervision.

Sales – "A new twist on sales." Sales trainers are a dime-a-dozen, and Avish is not one of them. Avish will show your sales force how to apply the art and science of improv to improve their ability to listen, gain rapport, think on their feet, ask better questions, and ultimately, make more money.

For more info:

www.AvishParashar.com
215-310-9263

Avish Parashar

Avish Parashar is an experienced, innovative, energetic, and humorous speaker who helps people and organizations get what they want through the art and science of improv. He uses his 15+ years of experience performing, directing and teaching improv comedy to deliver unique and refreshing presentations to a variety of audiences.

Weaving together humorous stories, jokes, audience interaction, and improv comedy games, Avish keeps the audience engaged while imparting key lessons around motivation, communication, and sales. By the end of one of Avish's presentations you will have key tools to flow with all that life throws at you.

Avish has spoken to the very creative (actors and directors), the very un-creative (accountants), the very casual (college students), and the very business-like (sales professionals). The end result is always the same -smiles, laughs, and a new way of looking at life and business.

70015657R00112

Made in the USA
Lexington, KY
09 November 2017